best | designed

hotels in europe

URBAN LOCATIONS

revised edition

Martin Nicholas Kunz

avedition lebensarr

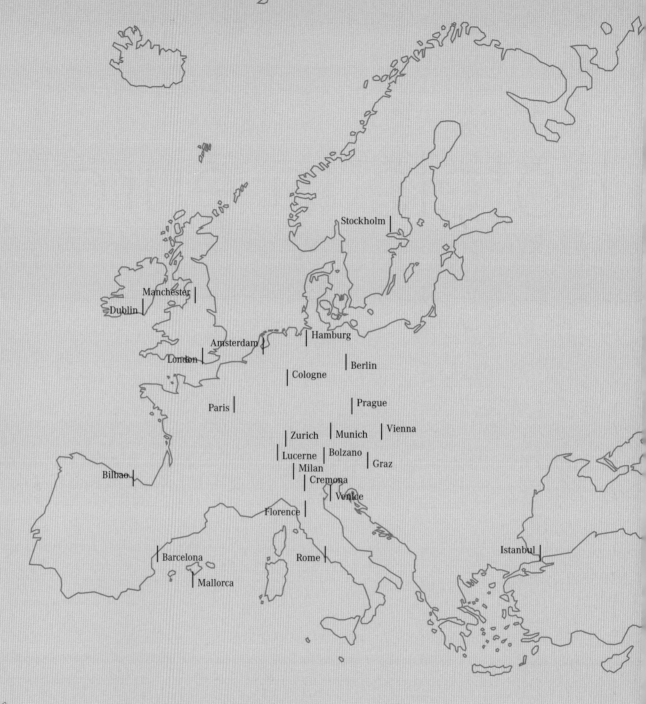

01 02

"Whenever I visit Florence and bite into a BigMac at McDonald's, I know I've come home". It was with this casual statement that a relatively well-known American architect saved a dying dinner conversation. Beforehand, his circle of friends was having a hard time discussing the benefits of a healthy diet and the role of the church in Asia. This was fine for a while, but when the ratatouille arrived, the conversation turned to art. Rhetoric and contradiction began to tangle themselves into ever more complicated knots, before reaching a crescendo of abstraction. One could sense the guests concentrating more and more on their food, and the time span between the "pop" of opening wine bottles began to get shorter. Boredom was approaching, until this statement lurched into the silence of the room.

Stunned faces. "You know what you've got", he continued. "Standardized, organised, quality controlled, high recognition value, clear positioning, fair prices. So why should I force down an overpriced and –let's face it – probably tasteless ciabatta with ham in a street café on a piazza?"

"But..." "And that's exactly what we're preaching and what we're trying to achieve: Global Corporate Identity – where everyone always knows what they're going to get."

"But..." "A CI that glows, that brings the company forward, that makes me, as a customer, feel safe, and this feeling of safety gives me comfort,"

"But..." "and comfort makes me feel that I've come home. It's as simple as that!"

"But there isn't a McDonald's in Florence!"

When this discussion took place many years ago, this was actually the case, the Renaissance town on the River Arno really had no McDonald's restaurant. But it was only a matter of time before the fastfood-chain began its triumphant march through Europe and, often against strong protest, decorated some of the continent's most historic places with its gleaming "Golden Arches". At a time when "globalisation" was not yet a bad word – it wasn't even actually a word – this brand logo indicated the beginning of the long and emotional conflict to come. Many, even at that time, prophesied the end of western European culture, fine style and individuality; destroyed under a barrage of American tastelessness.

But what really angered the spirits wanting to preserve this culture was, quite rightly and simply, a rather ugly logo destroying the balanced harmony of a Renaissance façade in Florence. American imperialist aspirations as an argument for rejection and rebellion appeared, at the most, in advanced political discussion.

The world had already eagerly accepted symbols of the American Way of Life – Coca-Cola and Jeans –with consumerist ease. Italians, Germans and the French were soon queuing up for a Quarter Pounder and fries. The tills rang, and are still ringing, the share price rose. It seems as though our architect had properly judged the instinct of the masses, even though he had never discovered the delights of a Big Mac himself. On leaving, he assured everyone that he was, in fact, a vegetarian, and found the ubiquitous "Golden Arches" an aesthetic crime. His provocative remarks, however, remained.

But his statement was, in essence and in terms of specific value, completely neutral. Later on, it was Italy that inspired a few young entrepreneurs in Seattle to replace the brown potion going by the name of "coffee" with "La Dolce Vita Italiana", in the shape of enjoyable espresso, cappucino or latte macchiato. If these boys had not appeared, as long-term planning market strategists, many Americans would never have got to know and appreciate a significant cultural treasure so intensely. Due to the quick spread of Starbucks, one can now even get decent coffee in the provinces.

But not only that: North-American coffee roasters are now attempting to bring their business beliefs back to the roots of their inspiration, by opening up branches in Europe. An American re-import of European values, so to say, which could be seen as almost embarrassing. Apart from the opponents of globalisation and despite the latent criticism of American cultural imports, this campaign did not encounter as much resistance as the hamburger fryers did. The reasons for this lie primarily in the spectrum of products. Which intellectual is going to start a protest against latte macchiato? The better design also had a positive effect, even if, in the end, it was applied according to the same recipe: standardized, organised, quality controlled, high recognition value, clear positioning and fair prices. This is regardless of whether we are talking Coca-Cola, McDonald's, Starbucks, Holiday Inn, Hilton, Hyatt or even the German hotel company Dorint.

Diametrically opposed to this standardized taste are an increasing number of committed entrepreneurs who, although often not from the industry, are developing a series of hotels that are distinguishable by unique design and a clear understanding of the local scene. With a combination of innovative ideas, creative concepts and more intimate sizes, this fresh niche has

06 | Modern travellers will find cosy lobbies...

07 | ... and personal, flexible service at the Reception Desk.

08 | The centre of attention: The lobby bar. Here, a puristic, clear atmosphere prevails in the Hotel Greulich...

09 | ...there, classic ambience with classy materials in the Radisson SAS Hotel Champs Elysées.

06   07

managed to succeed, above all in the lucrative, but demanding, business tourist market, created by the "Experience Economy".

For a long time this section went unnoticed or even ignored by the class of well-established hotels. But now even conservative companies have finally realised that young, international business leaders - and not only them – have different ideas on what travelling and short-term living and working in hotels should be about. With the caution, but also with the prudence of large companies, they first let the avant-garde test the market, which proceed to take over this rapidly growing niche with increasingly beautiful offers. They gained a positive feedback and, at last, success. Still, the hesitant attitude of hotel chains such as Hyatt, Dorint, Arabella Sheraton or Seaside paid off. Some years ago the target group was still considerably smaller and, more

importantly, its core preferred individual, owner-managed hotels with the greatest possible privacy and a personal atmosphere. Only a maximum of individualism and local colour was accepted, best of all with a host who would shake hands as if welcoming a friend. This type of guest was an outspoken scout for every kind of special aesthetic experience, for the extraordinary and the off-the-mainstream. The size of the target group grew along with the variety of such properties on offer, and the demands of this group widened too.

An adequate place to sleep in a clean room in a comfortable bed is no longer the credo but considered a basic. What has become more important now is the room size, the layout, the fittings, materials, furniture and accessories, as well as decoration. Anything goes, as long as there is a recognisable concept behind it – emotional and authentic.

Rooms can never be big enough, and layouts are well resolved. Smaller rooms look spacious and airy with the right lighting and as much daylight as possible. Examples include Gastwerk Hotel and Side, in Hamburg, where designers Florian Störmer and Matteo Thun, set standards by using transparency as the key concept. The same goes for Philippe Starck and the London Schrager Hotels: St. Martin's Lane and the Sanderson. The intelligent inclusion of daylight is part of the design, and is delivered by the use of floor to ceiling windows, mirrors for light re-direction and glass panels as room dividers. Another priority is the equipment of rooms with state-of-the-art technology. Today more than ever, hotel rooms are used for work and business meetings. Sufficient seating should be a basic item, and modem interfaces and power sockets should be close to the working spaces. Such necessities seem to be scarce, however, even in

well-planned hotels. Free-to-use computers, with internet access and printers, located in an agreeable atmosphere somewhere in the hotel are a good idea and desirable. At best, with a self-service espresso bar next to it, as is in the Paris Bel Ami.

Service amenities too, are essential for a hotel's success. Bars, restaurants and even wellness centres are important, if not in the hotel then certainly in the vicinity. Small hotels that do not offer these extras can have their own particular charm if the service is flexible enough for the needs of the modern traveller. Breakfast is important – quality, not quantity – and should be available at noon, or even around the clock.

All this requires a close eye on the market and the ability to translate user requirements into creative concepts. And success is not limited to avant-garde entrepreneurs, even if they were the instigators. Established corporations such as the Seaside Group and its Side Hotel, as well as the Dorint Group, with its hotels in Hamburg and Berlin drive forward this new hotel market, despite the watering down of the spirit of the original, in favour of standardisation and corporate identity. But corporate identity has its limits, and for hotel chains today, individuality and local flavour is just as important as good organisation, quality control, clear positioning and fair pricing.

Martin Nicholas Kunz

portixol | palma de mallorca . spain

DESIGN: Rafael Vidal, Christian Aronsen, Johanna & Mikael Landström

Perched on Portixol harbour, just a few minutes by scooter (the preferred mode of transport) from the port, this revitalised 1950's hotel could have easily been plucked from Miami's famous South Beach.

The Swedish owners have transformed the boxy shell into the most elegant hotel on the island. All that remains from the building's 1950's heyday is its simple façade, the original swimming pool and some interior mahogany detailing – the rest was completely gutted and rebuilt. However despite a complete overhaul to fresh, modern luxury, Portixol has managed to maintain a substantial portion of its 1950's charm. Some original furniture pieces from the period, including chairs and foot stools in the rooms, were restored and modernised by funky fabric. New furniture and finishes were carefully selected from all over Europe and beyond. Textiles imported from Holland, cutlery and glassware from Sweden and Finland, and custom designed furniture from Barcelona. Clean lines, chrome finishes, lots of white paint and pale wood spell Scandinavian chic. Attention has been paid to every detail: towels are soft and thick, bedlinen white and crisp and there are mountains of pillows to delve into. Views of the ocean are spectacular, as is the natural light that permeates through the building, with large panels of glass a feature of both the rooms and the lobby area.

The restaurant has regained the culinary reputation it held in the sixties and seventies when it started to steal the spotlight from the hotel, signalling the beginning of its decline. It is now once again considered by Mallorquins as the best seafood restaurant on the island, with innovative dishes and an exceptional wine cellar to match. The restaurant has an amazing copper roof that has already started to patina from the sea air. And if having the beach at the doorstep is too much to bear, the outdoor swimming pool and sun deck is a fine alternative. White American-style timber recliners sit poolside with simple stripped cushions for that casual seaside feel.

The sheer beauty, attention to detail, and breezy, summer atmosphere make Portixol a destination design hotel not to be missed.

01 | An icon of the 1950's – the original swimming pool and sun deck.

02   03   04

02 | Hotel guests and locals flock to one of the best seafood
restaurants on the island.

05 | View to the bath of a guest room.

03 | Reception area.

06 | Rooms are light and fresh – some with terraces and ocean views.

04 | Many of the original construction details have been restored and
supplemented with contemporary architecture.

07 | The cosy furnished lobby invites guests to tea time.

05

06 07

hotel claris | barcelona . spain

D E S I G N : Josep Martorell, Oriol Bohigas und David Mackay, MBM Architects

Even after the Summer Olympics of 1992, Barcelona remains one of the most beloved and creative cities in Spain – a place where the evening begins when people elsewhere have already gone to sleep. To enhance their personal stamina, a siesta is highly recommended for night owls. And perhaps no more a fabulous location exists for siesta-taking than poolside on the rooftop terrace of the Hotel Claris. Of course, one should first register as a guest, an undertaking that will prove exceptionally easy for anyone with a penchant for unusual hotels. After a five-year long renovation, the local architecture team of Josep Martorell, Oriol Bohigas and David Mackay (MBM Architects) created a hotel whose functional architecture handles history with abundant feeling while still progressing along entirely new pathways.

Only the Claris' Belle Époque façade, which supports the hotel while protruding beyond its recent additions, still remains of the urban palace originally built in 1892 as a Verduna Palace. Here, at the Hotel's angled corner, a clean termination forms, creating the intersection of the Pau Claris and Valencia.On the Claris' ground floor, solid glass window walls allow passers-by a rich view into the lobby, with its steel, glass and concrete dominated design. This view extends even to the lobby's rear, where a staircase and elevators, exposition rooms and restaurants are found. Among these spaces, the Claris' restaurant is most prominent, known for its "ampurdanic" kitchen with specialties from the Catalan Northwest.

Along with its stunning architecture, the Claris also contains its own archeological museum with one of the largest private collections of pre-Colombian artifacts in Spain. The collection is without doubt unique in the world and is actually a dominant theme throughout the Claris. Over 400 sculptures and paintings are distributed throughout the entire hotel – predominantly within its 124 rooms and suites. There, wooden floors and wooden inlaid walls are the dominant materials of the common areas, some of which extend up to two-stories in height. These and other elements form a warm interplay with pastel-coloured, textured walls to give the room a warm sense of atmosphere. The baths are luxuriously appointed with generous amounts of marble. And several suites even feature their own sauna and Jacuzzi.

01 | The roof terrace with pool and city panorama invites guests to take the ultimate siesta.

hotel claris | 13

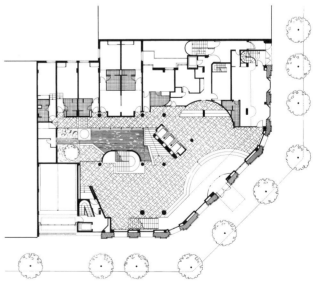

02 | View through the courtyard to the newly-designed façade.

03 | Dine like royalty over the roofs of Barcelona in "La Terraza" Restaurant.

04 | Pop Art meets Design at "East 47" Restaurant.

05 | Floor plan of the ground floor level.

06 | The torso of an ancient sculpture makes an attractive contrast to the clear lines of the staircase.

07 | Hallway with glass panes that look onto the courtyard.

08 | Seating arrangement in the lobby.

09 | Duplex Suite with classic leather furniture. A richly embroidered Chinese robe hangs on the wall.

prestige paseo de gracia | barcelona . spain

DESIGN: Josep Juanpere, GCA Arquitectos

The word 'prestige' originates from the French word meaning "illusion" or "glamour". In the English language, it means earned respect and admiration in the positive sense. The international design community, however, knows that, as of the summer of 2002, it has also taken on another meaning: This name stands for a leading hotel in the Spanish city of Barcelona. This dignified hotel has been completely modernised, yet still has a respectful relationship to the architecture of the Thirties. When examining the results of its renovation, one might be reminded of the image of tailored, refined threads. It is no wonder, because Josep Juanpere, the architect and designer, used many fabrics that promote a cool feeling for the new design.

The heart of the hotel is its marble staircase. It dates back to the founding of the hotel, and is still primarily in its original state. It not only optically connects the individual floors, it also holds together style and steel, wood and harmony in the building. But don't worry: No one has to climb stairs – just look at and admire them. All the climbing is done by the glass elevator, which brings guests to the five floors, past a large city map of Barcelona spread across the wall, complete with a little red lamp marking the Prestige. The new look is also evident in the 45 rooms of the design hotel. There, large photographs of Barcelona by Jorge Llorella hang on the walls. They are all 232 x 75 cm in size, and were made using the pinhole technique.

The interior decoration of the rooms is the work of the GCA Arquitectos architectural office. The designers were able to realise their visions of functionality, flexibility and fusion in a fantastic way. Some may consider it a paradox, others simply grand: From inside the hotel, one has a better and certainly more peaceful view of the city than from the Colón itself, one of Barcelona's landmarks. "To see and not be seen" might be the motto of those gazing with pleasure from the windows of the Prestige. Because behind the large wood and steel door to the foyer, another world can be found, one free of the bustle of the Catalonian city. The Prestige offers a special service in its so-called "Zeroom" – a kind of wellness lounge: the opportunity to listen to CDs of one's choice. In addition, the staff assists guests around the clock in selecting trendy shops or fashionable pubs and eateries in Barcelona.

02 03

04

02 | Anyone having a room with this view in the summer will feel like a king.

03 | A bathroom of the hotel.

04 | 06 The hotel's "Zeroom" promises pure relaxation.

05 | Beauty sleep à la Prestige.

07 | Those interested in designer shops will receive the appropriate addresses.

08 | The stylish staircase is only one of the many highlights in the hotel.

miró hotel | bilbao . spain

DESIGN: Antonio Miró

The Miró is situated in the centre of Bilbao, the delightful port city on the northern coast of Spain. The famous Guggenheim Museum is located only 200 metres away. Surrounded by so much art and Spanish history, it seemed logical to name the design hotel after the Spanish surrealist. An uncanny coincidence: well-known fashion designer Antonio Miró from Barcelona was responsible for decorating the 50 rooms and suites.

The interior of the Miró is pure theatre: Crème coloured leather sofas on deep black floors provide a stark contrast to the heavy satin drapes that serve in lieu of a wardrobe. Yet it is not these items that catch the guest's eye at first, although they are draped in a surprisingly unusual way, but the giant window frontage. They frame the play called "daily life", which the town's inhabitants improvise anew every day. From within, one is only part of the audience. The view from Rooms 82 and 83 on the eighth floor cannot be beat – it is hard to decide which is more gratifying: the warm water on all sides, or the old city sprawling at one's feet.

All corridors of the Miró reflect a devotion to art. An extensive photo collection by up-and-coming artists from the region is displayed next to works by internationally famous artists such as Alberto Peral. The hotel's friendly staff allows guests to forget the day's pressures, whether it be through getting a massage, relaxing in the Jacuzzi, the steam sauna or all of the above. Those preferring to clear their heads through sport will find satisfaction in the fitness area, furnished with the most modern equipment. Hotel guests and scene aficionados alike can find a pleasant close to the day in the bar, known for its cocktails. Those guests favouring to be alone but not wanting to do without entertainment will find a number of high-tech devices in their luxurious rooms: convenient flat screen televisions, CD players, or perhaps a film selected from the hotel's DVD library. Nevertheless: No technical gadget can beat the view from the gigantic panorama window.

01 | The giant window frontage of the Miró allows guests a magnificent view of Bilbao and the Guggenheim Museum.

02 03

04

05 | 06

02 | Beige and black are the predominant colours in the hotel.

03 | Detail of the upper level of the two-storey lobby.

04 | The Jacuzzi is the wellness oasis of this luxury hotel. Guests can
choose from a variety of offerings.

05 | One of the two conference rooms available at the Miró.

06 | Washbasin with a view. The glass dividers between bathroom
and sleeping area allow a view of what is going on in the room –
and beyond.

hotel bel ami | paris . france

DESIGN: Christian Lalande, Nathalie Battesti, Veronique Terreaux, Grace Leo-Andrieu

Just minutes from Boulevard St. Germain in the heart of Paris' chic Left Bank, Hotel Bel Ami has been designed with the young, fashion conscious crowd in mind. Housed in a converted 18th-century print factory, a recent refurbishment has transformed the hotel into a super stylish haven, replacing the bright colour and quirkiness of its former self with clean-lined modernism and subdued tones. And it's not just the hotel that will send fashion aficionados into a frenzy. The area of St. Germain des Prés, despite its traditional links with artists, intellectuals and radicals, is full of stylish boutiques and big name fashion houses such as Armani, Dior and Cartier. There is also an array of interesting galleries, cafés and antique shops to explore.

The site itself is shrouded in history that dates back well beyond its use as a print works. The new lobby of Hotel Bel Ami was once the west wing of Abbey St. Germain and the 14th-century monastery entrance used by Pope Alexander III. Two angels have been engraved into the hotel's stone façade as a symbolic reminder of its ecclesiastical past.

Today the lobby is an entirely different scene. Streamlined design provides a backdrop for the hotel's vibrant hub. Deep, comfortable sofas create a relaxed and informal atmosphere for residents and their guests. A selection of contemporary art and ceramics is on display and there are a number of rather stylish internet workstations, with coffee on hand from the nearby espresso bar. At the far end of the lobby is a separate fireplace lounge that can accommodate up to ten people for small presentations or meetings. It is also the perfect spot to unwind with the latest magazine or daily newspaper and the funky bar opposite is open for service well into the evening.

The 115 rooms and suites have been designed using a palette of caramel and anis green with accents of dark wood for wardrobes and bedheads. Cabinets have ample storage space to avoid clutter and satisfy the true minimalist. Bathrooms are classically simple with extensive use of white marble throughout. Breakfast is a must, even if it is just to check out The Cantine, located in the basement. The slightly decadent feel relates to its previous venue as the hotel's jazz club. Backlit flower prints hang on lilac walls and acid green leather sofas give the space an air of kitsch. A dramatic contrast to the underlying industrial theme. Designed by a team including architect Christian Lalande and interior designers Nathalie Battesti and Veronique Terreaux, the hotel refurbishment was overseen by Grace Leo-Andrieu. Appointed for her style and design flair, Leo-Andrieu has ensured that the new Hotel Bel Ami is certainly fit for the catwalk.

01 | Streamlined design and deep, comfortable sofas in the hotel's lobby lounge.

hotel bel ami | 25

02 03

04 | 05

02 | A palette of caramel and anis green with accents of dark timber define guest rooms.

03 | The fashionable reception area.

04 | Fresh colors in the breakfast room...

05 | ... and a self-serve espresso bar in the lobby are a good start-up for guest's business day.

pershing hall | paris . france

DESIGN: Andrée Putman

Cascades of tropical vines tumble from above. Ferns and exotic bushes spiral downward, embraced by grapevines and leaves – an interplay of light and green, shimmering in all possible nuances. All of that in the middle of Paris, a stone's throw away from the Champs-Elysées. The hanging gardens in the roofed courtyard constitute the centrepiece of Pershing Hall Hotel, a jungle that catapults guests into another world, created by design icon Andrée Putman. "It is the details that make the overall appearance beautiful," says the interior decorator, who imbued the stores of Karl Lagerfeld and Yves Saint Laurent with esprit, as she did previously with the rooms of the Cologne Hotel im Wasserturm or those of the New York Morgan Hotel. She transformed the upper-class Pershing Hall, rich in tradition, into a refuge for the contemporary elite. The atmosphere: a blend of modern art and completely exuberant ideas that are by no means ends in and of

themselves, but rather serve the hotel in every corner. John Pershing, after whom the hotel is named, would hardly recognise what awaits behind the façade, which dates back to the Second Republic. The US General (and you guessed it – namesake of the once disputed medium range missiles) used the building as living quarters during World War I. Yet, thankfully, only his name is reminiscent of that era.

Pershing Hall offers a mere 26 rooms and suites. There is no trace of mass production, no rote obsequiousness. The hotel is a prime example of infusing luxury with soul and expression – with an atmosphere feeding on colour, materials and décor. Speckled gauze decorates the windows in the rooms that look onto the tropical plant arrangement in the courtyard. The warm brown of the woods of which the side and coffee tables are made mingle harmoniously with the bronze

and moss hues and the white of the fabrics. The freestanding bathtub is the focal point of the bathrooms, resting on marble legs, surrounded by an ensemble of mirrors and refracting light. Whether one listens to the whispering of the colours or the softly passing time – guests here are sheltered in an interior tailored to all senses, as if in a dream-like setting, detached from the pulsating din of the Seine metropolis.

Those savvy in the Paris scene get together every evening in the lounge bar: A whisper of voices and music fills the room, and the city's DJ avant-garde invite all to a chill-out – which is especially recommended after having set your body's endorphins into motion in the hotel's newly opened fitness centre. Or, if when sipping on an aperitif, you wish to enjoy the feeling one only gets in the shadow of the Eiffel Tower: that of living like God in France.

01 | Modern art meets the Second Republic. In Pershing Hall Hotel, Andrée Putman perfects the harmony of opposites.

02 03

04

02 | Bathing like God in France:
     the freestanding bathtubs rest on
     marble legs.

03 | 04 Infusing luxury with soul: The
     interior of the 26 rooms and suites
     plays with the senses of the guests.

05 | In the lounge, you can listen to the time
pass. Right in the middle of Paris.

06 | A favourite meeting place, not only for
lunch: the roofed courtyard.

07 | Lighting arrangement in the foyer.

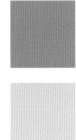

radisson sas hotel champs elysées | paris . france

DESIGN: Raymond Ichbiah, Gilles Leborgne, Ecart

The location in the eighth arrondissement selected by the Radisson SAS Group for their first hotel in Paris could not have been better: The golden triangle formed by the Champs-Elysées, Avenue Montaigne and Avenue Marçeau is home to everyone who is anyone in the established scene of designers: from Dior to Armani – nowhere is there a higher concentration of flagship stores, and the large star-earning restaurants are situated here, just as are the expensive, exclusive jewellers. In the narrow building on Avenue Marceau, with its typical Parisian Pierre de Taille façade and a view to the Arc de Triomphe, posh luggage maker Louis Vuitton once resided. Today, large round box trees in anthracite coloured metal pots of various heights mark the hotel's guest entrance.

The Parisian interior decorating office of Ecart created a contemporary style for the 46-room building that is emphatically serene, and thus has an excellent chance of enduring beyond the next few years without getting old. The selected hues of tobacco and honey contribute considerably to the effect. Along with the bleached oak parquet floors, they give character to the small lobby with an open fireplace, and can also be seen in the rooms, all kept in the same style. All furniture was designed for the hotel by Ecart. The velour covered easy chairs, with their curved wooden armrests, and the small round tables were inspired by art deco. All rooms are furnished with the latest technological equipment, such as flat screen monitors by Sharp, and guests can surf the Net wireless on their laptops anywhere.

The bathrooms are roomy, with their grey shimmering mosaic tiles and turquoise coloured friezes. There is only one single suite, which however has a magnificent roof terrace in teak. Framed by lightly scented lavender and laurel bushes, one can enjoy an excellent breakfast overlooking the rooftops of Paris. Jean-André Charial, head of the legendary "L'Ousteau de Baumanière" in Baux-de-Provence, serves as a consultant for the Restaurant La Place. With a menu that changes weekly, he endeavours to bring a piece of the Provence to Paris: This effort is especially successful in the shady terrace garden, where guests can enjoy a bouillabaisse en gelée and a lukewarm gâteau au chocolat under large white umbrellas.

01 | The shady terrace garden of the
Restaurant La Place, where provincially
inspired cuisine is served.

02 03

02 | Located above the rooftops of Paris, only a couple of steps away
from the Champs Elysées and the Arc de Triomphe.

03 | 04 Polished marble and columns mark the entry to the
restaurant. In the lobby with its tranquil, relaxed atmosphere,
small meals are also served.

05 | The only suite (Room 704) has a Jacuzzi and a roof terrace.

06 | Sparkling white sheets lighten the tobacco tones in the 45 rooms.

blakes hotel | amsterdam . netherlands

DESIGN: Anouska Hempel

Designed by Anouska Hempel, of London's Blakes and The Hempel fame, Blakes in Amsterdam is a toast to elegance and immaculate attention to detail. A combination of clean lines, comfort and symmetry, it is clear that every aspect of the design was undertaken with a great deal of care and consideration , coupled with an enormous amount of style.

The history of the building is remarkable and dates back to 1637 – the golden age when the Dutch East India Company was creating incalculable wealth and the new residential canals were the most sought after properties. Amongst these houses, the first theatre in the Netherlands was erected, quickly gaining the affection of artists, composers and European royalty. Tragically, about 120 years later, the building was burnt to the ground. All that remained were some stone arches and a sandstone porch – now the present day

doorway and guest check-in hall. Soon after the fire, the old foundations were rebuilt which saw the introduction of tall windows, marble entrance halls and delicate plasterwork, much of which remained unchanged until the recent transformation began. In its second incarnation, the building housed a bakery and during recent restoration work it was discovered largely intact. It is now the site of the Blakes restaurant.

The garden courtyard is a delightful enclave with tables and chairs placed in a perfect central line and sheltered by large umbrellas. Everything is tall due to the size of the space, including the clipped trees that line the perimeter. The brick wall surrounds have been oiled to create a dark brown glisten.Colour has been used with gusto in every room and schemes are inspired by exotic locations from around the world. There are those in black, grey and navy that the

designer refers to as 'Kimono', and others that are a combination of exotically named hues such as 'ginger' and 'turmeric', inspired by the Dutch East India Company. The 'elephant' and 'raspberry' rooms are another whimsical blend. Stripped sateen-finished fabrics dominate and Chinese antiques add an exotic, Asian touch. Rooms located off the courtyard are in the greens of lavender and rosemary, whilst those under the Dutch gables are understated beige and white. Hempel has taken the helm as both designer and management, overseeing every last detail. The blue and white plates in the restaurant are her design, and she directs the precise placement of glasses and sugar bowls on their individual square of slate. The food is also 'signature Hempel' – a stylised mixture of Japanese and Thai, devised not just for the flavours but also the colours and how it looks on the plate.

01 | The elegance of the hotel continues through to the intimate garden courtyard.

02 | The lobby and lounge areas are a combination of clean lines, symmetry and comfort

03 | 08 Symmetry is a major design aspect and is evident in the guest rooms, all of which have a different colour scheme and layout

04 | Even the potted plants are a bit different in this hotel.

05 | The historical building fabric has been tenderly preserved and combined with modern furniture.

06 | Black and white make up the prevalent contrast – even for the lobby seating.

07 | A view into the restaurant.

04 05
06
07 08

51 buckingham gate | london . united kingdom

DESIGN: Dan Nelson, Noel Pierce

It is quite possible that the Queen and Prince Charles steal envious looks in the direction of 51 Buckingham Gate: Only two minutes by foot from their abode, almost within view of Buckingham Palace, stand the luxurious suites and apartments of that hotel, built in the year 2000, in which the comfort of a majestic lifestyle is combined with the elegance of prize-winning design, as well as the intimacy of an establishment that makes its guests' privacy its top priority. Since its opening, 51 Buckingham Gate has been considered one of the best accommodations in London – as discreet as it is noble, it is magnificent, but never gaudy. In a word: sophisticated.

British understatement is evident right at the door: A plain blue baldachin marks the entrance to this Taj Hotel, which looks rather inconspicuous from the outside. New arrivals drive up in a chauffeured limousine that transfers guests from one of the airports or railway stations to Westminster. The check-in: variable, so that VIPs do not have run-ins with lurking paparazzi. In the hotel, guests enjoy the Ivor Spencer Butler Service, the first of its kind on the island: While liveried servants tend to the luggage, guests have the opportunity to explore their rooms, to which interior decorators Dan Nelson and Noel Pierce have lent their distinctive flair. The deluxe and superior suites have up to five bedrooms, offering plenty of room for relaxation and contemplation. The finely-tuned interiors form their own continuum, suite for suite: classic and unpretentious – harmonising in their precise composition of colour, furniture and materials; some diffusing a fresh atmosphere in white, blue and black, and others displaying a warm ensemble of brown, ochre and beige. Woods and fabrics emphasise the unobtrusive tone of the design, which has garnered a series of prizes – including laurels for the exquisite bathroom design, which seamlessly incorporates rustic elements, such as washing bowls, with an air of contemporary beauty. The most spectacular suite is without a doubt the Prime Minister's Suite, which is sure to catch the fancy of more than just heads of state: an exceptionally noble accommodation that makes guests want to apply for permanent asylum.

Private dining is possible in all suites – 24 hours a day, and even in the form of a dinner party, for which the hotel's chef prepares epicurean feasts. Or you can order fish & chips, depending on your mood. A visit to the Bank Westminster and the Zander Restaurant is also worthwhile, even for its 48-metre bar alone – the longest in Europe. Divided into two dining rooms seating 20 persons each, the restaurant enables uninterrupted enjoyment: The flavours of contemporary cuisine can be savoured in a private atmosphere.

01 | Award-winning design: Noel Pierce
created the bathrooms in London's new
top accommodation.

02 | The charm of Buckingham Gate is in the details.

03 | The atmosphere: sophisticated.

04 | An intimate atmosphere in the heart of London – starting at the reception desk.

05 | British lifestyle: noble, but not gaudy.

06 | The hotel's guests have the city's treasures at their feet.

07 | Classic and unpretentious – the design at 51 Buckingham Gate.

08 | A warm ensemble of colour and materials in the luxury suites.

07

08

Continental breakfast, as well as tea and cocktails, can be had in the hotel's own library, for the exclusive use of its guests.

In the Shiseido Qi Salon, guests can take refuge from appointment pressures and workday stress. Upon request, visitors can be assisted by personal trainers; if needed, nannies will watch the little ones, so everyone can make the most of their stay without worries. Staying at 51 Buckingham Gate? It's more than just an accommodation – it's a royal delight.

great eastern hotel | london . united kingdom

DESIGN: Sir Terence Conran, James Soane (CD Partnership), Manser Associates

The area surrounding the city of London has recently emerged as one of the British capital's most important destinations for forward thinking hoteliers ever since Gordon Campbell Gray transformed a former newspaper headquarters and Lloyd's bank into One Aldwych in 1998. Then followed the entrée of hotel guru, Ian Schrager, with St Martins Lane in late 1999 and, soon after, his Sanderson sensation. Terence Conran then arrived on the scene with his design for the Great Eastern Hotel right next to Liverpool Street Station.

As the only hotel actually within the one square mile that defines London's City, the Great Eastern holds a coveted position in this well-established financial and social sphere – a position bolstered by the hotel's architectural and functional history. Built in 1884 for the Great Eastern Railway Company to designs by Charles Barry, the hotel

was intended as a luxurious end point for the elite train passengers disembarking at Liverpool Street Station. It was extended in 1901 by Colonel Robert Edis, prompted by an increase in continental traffic.The hotel originally contained 136 rooms, but now extends to 267 following the $100 million renovation. Despite the recent expansion, the Great Eastern's original early Renaissance, classically Victorian façades remain intact. What has also remained is the hotel's tradition of luxury accommodation for its mobile, moneyed clientele.

While visitors today are more likely to arrive via jumbo jet rather than steam train, they are still accommodated with the same sense of privileged pampering, style and service. In keeping with the hotel's locale, furniture is covered in fabrics traditionally used for business suits, bed valances have a tailored, cufflink detail, towels and sheets

are monogrammed and custom woven 'tweed' carpet graces the corridors. Additional pieces from classic designers such as Eames, van der Rohe and Jacobson as well as contemporary contributions from Conran, complete the Great Eastern's modern take on classic, British lodging. Refreshingly, bathrooms move away from the ubiquitous marble finishing. Instead, clean white tiles and Victorian tap fittings combined with ultra-deep baths and cabinets reminiscent of The Orient Express give a cabin effect and are a modern take on the now obsolete mode of travel. The architects have created a large void – which is referred to amongst hotel staff as their own 'Mini-Guggenheim' – to link the two buildings and provide a central point of reference. This feature is the most prominent manifestation of the design brief: to introduce modern design alongside the revival of the classic. This space is also fittingly utilised for exhibitions or as a gallery

01 | 'Mini-Guggenheim' is the nickname of the area designed to link the two buildings and is often used for changing art exhibitions.

space, servicing the ongoing partnership with galleries in the area and local artists in nearby burgeoning quarters of creativity such as Hoxton and Shoreditch. The hotel boasts a number of interesting and varied eating and drinking venues, including its fine dining restaurant, Aurora, the ever-buzzing Terminus and George – a modern take on the traditional English pub. There is also a seafood restaurant, champagne bar and a Japanese sushi bar.

02 | View down to the atrium.

03 | 05 The entrance lobby with period detail from its previous life.

04 | Rooms at the Great Eastern are a modern take on classic, British lodging.

06 | Aurora, the hotel's fine dining restaurant, combines old and new in perfect harmony.

04

05 06

metropolitan | london . united kingdom

DESIGN: Keith Hobbs, Linzi Coppick (United Designers)

In the fashionable London district of Mayfair, tastemaker Christina Ong is helping the city retain its claim as a premier design and fashion destination. Having already established herself as the owner of the Halkin hotel, Ong displays her love of detail once again here at the Metropolitan. "Take a piece of paper and design me a hotel that precisely satisfies the desires and needs of business travellers," – that was Ong's charge to her hotel's British architects, Keith Hobbs and Linzi Coppick. Unsurprisingly, the Metropolitan's 115 rooms and 18 suites have been arranged with maximum attention to service, simple furnishings, and logical in-room features such as ISDN lines, fax machines and modem connections.

The furniture also has a similar, individual approach to living, and was made especially for the hotel out of warm, reddish pear wood. The cushions, blinds, curtains and carpets have also been crafted out of pure, natural materials. With such a level of high-design planning, nothing appears "set up". Instead the rooms emit a strong simplicity, one that begins in the lobby, where calming in-house music serves as an auditory retreat from the noise outside.

The Metropolitan's architecture has an air of the contemporary about it, but remains utterly timeless. While its main spatial configurations could easily have been designed in the 1920s, its overall aesthetic could equally be imagined as a vision of the future, an aesthetic that even applies to the employee uniforms, which originate from the studio of Donna Karan. Perhaps the Metropolitan is to hotel architecture what DKNY is to fashion: practicality, elegance, comfort and simplicity.

Along with its Park Lane location in the heart of London, the Hyde Park views from most of the hotel's rooms are also highly coveted, as is Nobu, actor Robert de Niro's Japanese kitchen, located on the second floor. Its light, sumptuous menu is easy to digest, while still providing enough energy for after-dinner drinks at the nearby Met Bar, and later a dip into London's fashion scene after the city's 11pm closing time.

01 | The lobby: In spite of the loft-like spaciousness there's an intimate ambience. The clock with its Sgraffito numbers is an immediate eye-catcher.

02 03

04

05

06

no. 5 maddox | london . united kingdom

DESIGN: John Pawson

Running between London's Bond Street and Regent Street and surrounded by the fine shops and the buzz of the metropolis is quiet little Maddox Street. Hidden away at number 5 is a small, bijou hotel, in the broad sense of the word, although "living rooms" – the term used by the hotel itself – is far more appropriate for this simple brick building with its chic serviced apartments. "Do your own thing" is the key, an opportunity for visitors to make this their "home from home" in the big city.

The idea behind the company philosophy is for guests to do as they please – hold a meeting in their own suite or cook for themselves in their private kitchen. Who needs public spaces anyway when your very own city-center domicile awaits with bamboo plants and aromatic stones for relaxation? The name of the game here is laid back, with twelve suites (one with its own planted terrace) providing an oasis of calm. Guests staying in the deluxe suite may opt for settling down in front of an open fire or escaping to the covered balcony with a good book.

Being a small hotel, it has no gym. But the designers chose to omit the lift, giving the guests an alternative form of exercise with access to their suites via a sweeping staircase. First, check-in has a "welcome gift" for all new arrivals, a generous starter pack of groceries provided by the hotel for use in the guests' own kitchen. If cooking does not appeal, a round-the-clock food service means there is no chance of going hungry. The Big Bar menu lists "good" and "bad" options, ranging from snacks like "good" miso soup and Yogi tea to "less good" gin and Ben and Jerry's ice cream. Guests preferring to eat out do not even need an umbrella – the building's basement has the Patara, one of the best Thai restaurants in town. Which is saying something. Its atmosphere matches that of the hotel: a modern balance of European-Asian design influenced by Ou Baholydhin.

Despite its size, No. 5 Maddox Street caters for virtually any technological need guests might have. Workstations with voicemail, fax and ISDN modem facilitate communications with the business world outside. And if, at some point, the bed proves irresistible, there is the added luxury of Abe Hamilton kimonos and faux-sable bed throws. So that, the next morning, the discovery tour of the capital can continue on one of the bicycles provided by the hotel.

02 03

02 | Asian-inspired design that stirs the
senses.

03 | The living areas are designed with a
view to detail and relaxation.

04 | Dining area. All suites are equipped
with a kitchen, allowing guests the
option of cooking for their guests
themselves.

05 | As a gesture of welcome, the managers
fill the kitchen with all sorts of treats –
including champagne.

06 | Deluxe backyard retreat. This terrace
with greenery belongs to one of the
suites.

04
05 06

threadneedles hotel | london . united kingdom

DESIGN: GA Design

Even the exterior of this hotel in London's traditional banking heartland cuts a striking impression, its stout walls and classic Victorian façade concealing a history going back almost a hundred and fifty years. The building began life as the Midland Bank's London headquarters and later became the prestigious address of the Merchant Taylor Company. If only for the sake of reputation, its owners left behind a good deal of visible evidence of their capital assets, traces that were not just erased when the building was converted into a new luxury hotel. Inside the hotel, the fact that the cogs in the wheels of history continue to turn and interlock with a certain sense of inevitability is a source of fascination in itself. 'Threadneedles', the name of the hotel, is apposite, for it resembles a canvas in which architecture intended for show is interwoven with decor that has all the freshness of modern design.

Guests entering the center of the foyer find themselves greeted by what was the centerpiece of the building in its heyday: a huge glass dome that bathes the former banking hall in a shimmering blue light. This atrium-like reception area is surrounded by marble pillars and ceilings with stucco decoration. Just sinking into the dark red leather armchairs here brings a sense of that bygone era when money was the leading player here, while Russian tea is served with the utmost discretion.

However, these echoes of the interior design and culture of the past are complemented by decidedly neo-modern details and lighting, especially in the hotel corridors and hallways. Rooms and suites are in the quintessential traditional English style, but also have a contemporary feeling of clarity and simplicity. Bathrooms impress with their combination of limestone, attractive glass

partitions and elegant accessories of polished chrome. As befits a building where everything once revolved around money, no expense has been spared in creating a hotel which offers the ultimate in luxury and tranquility. Alongside all the usual technical support services for modern business communications, it also offers especially respectful and attentive service. Evidently setting great store by its high standards in this area, the hotel also displays a very palpable, typically English reserve. In a nutshell, it is a blend of tradition, zeitgeist and refinement – which also goes for the cuisine served in "Bonds", the hotel's restaurant.

01 | The large, lavishly decorated glass-domed roof is the heart and the jewel of the foyer.

02 03

04

02 | Sleek, modern forms meet Victorian
pomp in the lobby.

03 | Between magnificent columns and
under the gentle light of the glass dome,
the distinguished leather easy chairs
present an ideal spot for an evening
drink.

04 | An abundance of dark wood lends the
rooms a noble, British atmosphere.

05 | View into the restaurant.

06 | Floor-to-ceiling panelling behind the
beds adds an expressive touch.

eleven didsbury park | manchester . united kingdom

DESIGN : Sally O'Loughlin

One of the first hotels in Manchester to have a design focus, Eleven Didsbury Park is aptly referred to as a contemporary townhouse hotel. A hundred and fifty years old dilapidated mansion was converted into a stylish boutique hotel by owner Eamonn O'Laughlin and his interior designer wife, Sally. Together they have produced a perfect accommodation solution for the bustling business centre in England's northwest.

Each of the 14 rooms are individually designed and furnished using contemporary pieces custom-made by Scottish and Irish craftsmen. White walls provide a neutral background to a palette of rich tones, evident in textiles and timber. Beautiful padded-fabric bedheads and luxurious quilted bed covers in colours of aubergine, pecan and assam create a sense of the exotic. It's not only the architecture and design that gives this hotel its charm. Its owners ensure that

there is every modern convenience as well as the kind of personal service that was "taken for granted 100 years ago." A secluded walled garden at the rear of the building is for the exclusive use of guests. Perfect for a game of croquet or quiet drink in its peaceful surrounds. In the summer months, enjoy the alfresco dining on the barbeque terrace.

The hotel is a welcome addition to Didsbury's thriving and cosmopolitan restaurant scene. There are plenty of great places to eat but until Eleven's arrival, these were never matched with the right kind of hotel. For those who prefer to dine in, the hotel offers a simple deli-style menu of pasta, sandwiches and light snacks. The Irish breakfasts are enormous and not to be missed.

01 | View of the breakfast room. On the
walls, collages made of silverware.

02 03

04

05 06

02 | The large garden entices guests to relax in style.

03 | Seating arrangement in the reception area.

04 | Old furniture can hold its own amid the contemporary design.

05 | The relaxed atmosphere also allows room for informal business meetings.

06 | The colour scheme of the beds adds an expressive touch to the rooms.

the morrison hotel | dublin . ireland

DESIGN: John Rocha, Douglas Williams

The Morrison is one of the most luxurious and visually stunning hotels in Europe. A collaborative effort of designer Douglas Wallace and fashion dynamo, John Rocha, it is a masterpiece of thoroughly modern concepts behind an 18th-century Georgian façade. This imposing, south-facing townhouse overlooks Dublin's River Liffey and is a combination of contemporary and oriental influences. Unique in concept as far as conventional Dublin hotels go, The Morrison still manages to pay homage to its Irish heritage. Highly acclaimed Rocha, was asked to design all of the interiors, furnishings and fabrics for the hotel in his first interior commission. The brief was to create a stylish, contemporary hotel that was primarily Irish. Local artists were used to paint all of the 140 paintings that adorn the walls of public spaces and rooms alike. Artefacts from the east were sourced specifically, fabrics were hand painted and sculptures commissioned.

The interior is a mix of high ceilings with pale white walls, stone floors and beautiful grey hand crafted Irish carpets. Leather and silk, velvet and linen are just some of the sensual textiles used throughout. Other luxurious finishes and objects are evident including an impressive gold leaf painting, commissioned specifically for the project, that frames the reception area. Opposite are heavy, imposing mirrors tilted against the wall giving the desk an altered perspective.

Religious overtones are prevalent in the cathedral-like space of the hotel restaurant, Halo. Artwork displays a distorted cross, a dramatic 'theatrical' staircase leads from the ground to the skies, and vast lengths of weighty black velvet hang as a room divider between kitchen and dining room. Chef Jean-Michel Poulot makes artful presentation of the food, which has a cosmopolitan edge. His philosophy is to work with the finest of Irish

ingredients, respecting the natural flavours through careful preparation.

The Morrison has 84 of the most stylish and comfortable rooms in the city. Soothingly monochromatic in black, chocolate and cream, each with a hint of the calm of the Orient; from the luxurious velvet painted throws across crisp white Frette linen to the simplistic calm of a delicately placed, floating lily inside a crystal bowl. Walls are curved where bedroom meets bathroom. Floors are cool limestone and walls are intricate mosaics. Luscious fragrant products for pampering display thoughtful attention to detail. The basement is home to one of the hotel's bars and is themed by art, sculpture and warm, inviting colours. Lights are encased in whimsically woven rattan, creating amazing spider web reflections on walls, and seats are upholstered in red ponyskin.

01 | A classic atmosphere of brown tones in the rooms, combined with accents of beige and black.

02　03

02 | Hotel lounge. Commissioned artworks are an integral part of the hotel concept.

03 | 05 Paintings, sculpture and warm inviting colours define the hotel's bars and restaurants.

04 | Fashion designer John Rocha chose a pure and elegant mix of materials and colour.

04 | 05

berns hotel | stockholm . sweden

DESIGN: Olle Rex, Anders Björkén, Terence Conran

A Scandinavian beauty even from afar, its historical façade, framed by statuettes and adornments, is dominated by high rounded arch windows that reflect Stockholm's city lights. The front of the hotel, a series of rising terraces, softens the appearance of the building and gives it a certain delicateness and dignity. Not a cold, Nordic feel – quite the opposite. As soon as guests step inside the glass rotunda, they immediately sense an ambience that blends the chic of a bygone era with the welcome aspects of contemporary design.

The name Berns has been a familiar one to the people of Stockholm since the 19th century. Heinrich Robert Berns, originally from Germany,

opened a "Swiss café" here in 1863. Known as "Berns Salon" – part variety theatre, part café-restaurant – it attracted artists from all over the world, with acts ranging from a Chinese fire-eater to composer Paul Lincke and singers Josephine Baker and Edith Piaf. Over the course of 120 years, the building underwent one series of alterations after another. Then, in 1989, there emerged the new Berns Hotel, designed by architect Olle Rex. A charming hotel in a central location beside Berzelii Park, it has 61 rooms and four individually designed suites (the largest with its own private sauna). The interaction between cherry wood, marble and the warm tonal interior creates an atmosphere that is discreet, personal and never overbearing.

In spring 2002, the top floor of the hotel – the five deluxe rooms with their private balconies or terraces overlooking the park, Nybroviken bay and Strandvägen – was given a total makeover by interior designer Anders Björkén. The decor combines understated elegance and exquisite materials and is complemented by contemporary paintings by Peter Hammar which hang in all the rooms. For business travelers, Berns Hotel has its own business center and conference hall. All rooms have a fax connection and internet access.

As well as offering accommodation, the Berns Hotel is also one of Stockholm's top gastronomic addresses. The lounge, designed by Terence

01 | View of the lounge designed by Terence
Conran: the interior combines 19th-
century elegance with modern-day
comforts.

02 03

Conran, is a stunning example of how to combine the traditional and the modern. Carved wooden ceilings, majestic chandeliers and baroque façade work are juxtaposed with sober bar structures with frosted glass fronts and plain upholstery. Rooms overflow, one into the next: from the lounge to the restaurant, the cocktail

bar and the wine bar to the LE nightclub on the floor below. LE, which means 'smile' in Swedish, is completely bathed in red, but add the brilliant white of the spotlights and you have a mood mix that combines Moulin Rouge and ice floe. An ambience that appeals so much that, at weekends, standing in line for hours is all part of the party.

02 | Openness and grandeur of design at Berns Hotel.

03 | Flowing forms and warm colors in the 65 rooms and suites.

04 | Each room has its own special character.

05 | The cocktail bar, where the cream of Stockholm society gets together.

06 | Foyer seating.

07 | Theatre-style conference hall.

04 05

06 07

hotel j | stockholm . sweden

DESIGN: Peter Ågren (Millimeter), Klas Litzén (R.O.O.M.), Nyrén

For the most memorable arrival, Hotel J is best accessed by boat – a fifteen-minute journey from downtown Stockholm. Situated right on the water at Nacka Strand, the hotel has underlying references to sailing and its waterside location.

The main hotel building is a short walk up the pier. Once inside, a contemporary marine style is immediately apparent, with interiors reminiscent of a Rhode Island beach house. The lobby is much like a living room and consists of a reception area, breakfast room and lounge. An open fireplace – boasting the stars and stripes banner above, confirming the American inspiration – combined with stunning water views over the Royal Djurgården, Lidingö and boats on Saltsjön,

make it the natural and relaxing meeting place for guests and visitors. Two new wings have been added to accommodate the hotel's 45 generous sized rooms, some have a balcony or patio and others are split-level. The name 'J' has been derived from a sailing term used in the America's Cup of the 1930s and reflects the underlying maritime theme. Every finish, furnishing and detail has been carefully selected to reflect the waterside location.

Rooms are light and airy, with walls painted crisp white. Lengths of blue and white striped fabric have been used for quilts, curtains and cushions. Loose-covered, comfortable chairs are anchored to the space by patterned floor rugs. Pale timber

furniture and detailing is interspersed and polished black floorboards are a fitting contrast.

Restaurant J is situated on the pier by the water and its design, much like the hotel, is inspired by east coast American boathouses. In the summer months, guests can relax on the jetty and enjoy the sunshine and scenery from the smart wooden recliners that sit neatly around the perimeter.

01 | Nautical blue and white, as well as
warm woods, colour the furnishings.

02 03

02 | A terrace in front of one of the two new
wings with a view of the skerries.

03 | Breakfast room and lobby with an open
fireplace.

04 | Connecting walkway between the old
and new building.

05 | Mundane seaside resorts of the east
coast of the USA, with their sailing
traditions, provided the inspiration for
the design concept.

06 | The bright, airy rooms free your mind.

07 | A generous breakfast buffet in a relaxed
atmosphere provides for a positive start
to the day.

ROOM
10–18

04 05
06 07

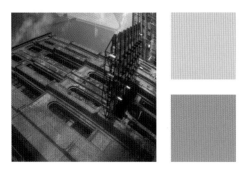

gastwerk | hamburg . germany

DESIGN: Peter Lange (Volgler, Lange und Partner), Regine Schwethelm, Sybille von Heyden

'Gaswerk' is the german word for 'gasworks', a power station providing a power-hungry city with energy. Now, however, 'Gaswerk' will forever boast a new meaning with the opening of the Gastwerk (gast = guest) hotel in Germany's northern port metropolis of Hamburg. Created from the hulk of a former power station, the Gastwerk is Germany's first "loft-style" hotel.

Each of its 135 rooms and suites are spacious and airy, reflecting the grandeur of the structure's former function while also containing modern comforts such as TV, VCR, CD-players and Internet access. Architect Klaus Peter Lange along with designers Behlmann & Schwethelm have incorporated organic materials and subtle, natural tones into each room's overall aesthetic which is centred around large beds, spacious bathrooms and unobtrusive furnishings to keep the space open and accessible. Being so close

to Hamburg's city centre – and in fact the centre for much of Germany's media industry – the Gastwerk is also well-placed to serve as a small, intimate corporate retreat or headquarters for visiting executives. A 400 square metre conference area conforms to the same open-planned design found in the Gastwerk's rooms, a look which is facilitated by the hotel's high windows and ample sunlight. The conference space is equipped with state-of-the-art technology, featuring video-displays and ISDN outlets. The larger conference space is just one of a dozen different meeting spaces beginning at 50 square metres – all of which provide access to a nearby business lounge for meeting breaks.

For those looking for more of a respite from the business world, the Gastwerk provides a slew of recreational and relaxation activities to calm even the most frayed nerves. A sauna – designed with

a nod to the Orient – is a centre of calm within the hotel, while the Italian restaurant, bar and winter garden serve as low-key, yet luxurious, meeting points at the end of the day. There's even on-site parking for easy access to urban auto adventures late into the night.

01 | The high lobby, with atrium, is unique
in Hamburg. It is divided into different
segments and strewn with art objects.

02 | 03

04

02 | Seating arrangement in the lobby.

03 | The rooms are connected by lifts and gallery walkways.

04 | Very relaxed: the bright lounge.

05 | The renovated arched windows are especially beautiful, and, together with the red brick walls, lend many rooms their loft-like character.

06 | A view from outside through historical, glazing bar-studded windows into the bar.

07 | The Asian Relaxing Zone, with its sauna and solarium, is designed to refresh tired bodies.

05 | 06

07

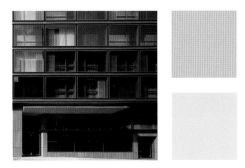

side hotel | hamburg . germany

DESIGN: Jan Störmer (Alsop Störmer Architekten), Mattheo Thun, Robert Wilson

Appealing to the modern, urban generation, Side Hotel is located close to the opera house, theatre, shopping area and central business district of Hamburg. A striking combination of glass and stone, extending over 12 storeys and surrounding 180 rooms, is the signature feature of the building, designed by German architects Alsop & Störmer. Such a structure enabled an atrium-style lobby reaching 24 metres high which creates an unusual interior space with an overwhelming impact on arriving guests.

The architects' concept was the development of a solidium, where a sculptural spine and an inserted glass aisle fit together to form a whole. Because of such a building composition, each room is different and has varying light reflexes. The upper three floors have the most amazing views across Hamburg's rooftops. To complement the architecture, Milan designer Matteo Thun

created the interiors. Thun, referred to as a designer of everyday cultures, challenges the visitor to a completely revised way of thinking, seeing and experiencing things. Minimalism – 'a reduction to the essentials' – is his fundamental approach to the interior. Right down to the ashtrays and toothbrush holders, every piece of furniture and decorative element has been selected or developed as part of the concept.

Dark wooden floorboards, furniture and wall units are integrated with lighter coloured fabrics, opaque glass and stainless steel. Chocolate brown throws and cushions adorn the crisp white linen and white padded and buttoned headboards are part of the dark timber bed surround. Such applications bring together a range of interesting textures in the clean-lined rooms. The Flying Suites on the 11th and 12th floor are a symphony of white minimalism and

elegance, with slick bathrooms becoming one and the same space as the sleeping area.

The foyer itself is a visual feast. Light installations by New York light choreographer Robert Wilson are an outstanding feature of the lobby and give the space a sense of excitement. Changing, computer controlled lighting impulses enable changes of mood over the course of the day, according to the seasons or weather conditions. Such interrelation of space and light defines the hotel interior.

The Side bar, Fusion, is entirely red – a complete contrast to the rest of the hotel. Various function rooms and lounges throughout offer an array of communication centers for guests and visitors.

01 | The atrium, eight storeys high, is an architectural marvel. Its impressive glass structure features work by New York light choreographer, Robert Wilson.

02 03

02 | One of Hamburg's hot spots – the hotel restaurant, offering east-meets-west cuisine.

03 | Washbasin in a WC.

04 | The hotel's vibrant bar, Fusion.

05 | Glass is the dominant material in the bathrooms.

06 07

08

09

06 | Sketch of the upper eight floor lounge.

07 | The wellness area with swimming pool, sauna steam bath and gym.

08 | Behind coloured furniture designed by Matteo Thun for Side is the illuminated glass wall atrium.

09 | 12 The terraces above the 8th floor in a design sketch, and in reality.

10 | Conference corner on the 8th floor.

11 | Entrance to the wellness area.

13 | Different window configurations and dark timber floors differentiate the back rooms from the front.

10 11

12 13

dorint am gendarmenmarkt | berlin . germany

DESIGN: Harald Klein, Bert Haller – K/H Büro für Design und Innenarchitektur

The success of well-designed hotels has inspired the Dorint-Group for some time. With the transformation of a concrete slab building from the 1980s, the Dorint am Gendarmenmarkt is positioned in a top location for aesthetics-lovers in the historical yet new centre of Berlin. It is not only the interior design that is a pleasure for the eye; the neighbouring area is ideal terrain for all architecture aficionados. The surroundings are full of new and historically relevant buildings, museums and galleries. Equally, there are endless shopping possibilities, excellent restaurants and bars as well as political institutions such as the Reichstag, all within walking distance.

This spot opposite the French Chathredral inspired the designers Harald Klein and Bert Haller to fuse German and French stylistic elements in their creation. The task was not a simple one. They had to do justice to the listed buildings within the old ensemble, take on historical elements and add modern ones. "A design that inspires one to think. One that enables the history of a room to be read and that makes living in it a sensual experience", say the planners. With its 92 rooms and suites, the five-star hotel is still compact enough to allow a personal atmosphere. Independent of their size the rooms are furnished simply, practically and comfortably.

The interior mainly consists of specifically designed fittings. The cupboard space has been kept in light colour tones whilst the storage areas and large desk surfaces are dark. Light and shade alternate in an exciting rhythm strongly supporting the effect of the room. Several rooms on the upper floors have their own balcony and a view onto the French Chathredral. In addition to attracting sophisticated metropolitan tourists, the hotel is designed to primarily attract business travellers who enjoy a feeling of individuality. Thus it is also suitable for conferences, seminars and congresses. Up to 160 people can be seated in the five event rooms. The "Delphinium" auditorium, with its illuminated glass floor, is ideally suited to events or product launches.

A fitness and wellness area complete with sauna, steam bath, open-air terrace and extended chill-out zone balance out mental exertions. Situated over two attic floors, it is a vision of white colour and minimal design. Gastronomically, the Artrium Cafe and the Restaurant Aigner welcome their guests – both areas accentuated with a rational-modern design and displaying the quality expected of a luxury hotel.

01 | Light and shadows play. Timelessly elegant seating arrangement in the lobby.

02 03
04 05

06 | 07

08

02 | Reception area with a historically modernist décor.

03 | Sleek lines characterise the design – with a concentration on the essential.

04 | Delphinium banquet hall with fully equipped conference and stage technology.

05 | Lounge chairs in the wellness area above the roofs of Berlin.

06 | Atrium Café. Behind its columns, guests will find an impressive breakfast buffet.

07 | Suite with a view of the French cathedral.

08 | Business room with balcony.

ku'damm 101 | berlin . germany

DESIGN: Kessler + Kessler, Kadel Quick Scheib, Vogt + Weizenegger, Lemongras

"Bags unpacked, am on 4th floor, and you?" After a short pause, a metallic "You've got mail" is heard from Room 207 on the second floor: "I am here too… Want to meet afterwards in the bar?" The 4th floor answers: "Have to download a few files first – by the way: have you showered yet?" Room 207: "Yes, nice big shower head. What do you think of the décor?" 4th floor: "Modest, but good, especially the colours – have you read that they are the colour sequences of Le Corbusier?" Room 207: "Perhaps a bit bare, but…when are we going to the bar, anyway? Wait, I've just got an email from Room 301"… Just how long this exchange of emails from bed to bed via the hotel network went on is a mystery. Those guests never did show up at the bar, not

on that evening. At some point, their comfy mattresses undoubtedly freed them from their LANs and WANs and transported them into deep sleep. So deep that they most likely did not even hear the unmistakable steps on the rubber floors of the hallways. "We had a small budget, but we did splurge on the mattresses," verifies Jens Gmiat. The hotel director raves about the power of good ideas that cost little money, and praises the overall design concept of the Zurich office of Kessler+Kessler. "They simply combined mostly low-cost furnishings and accessories in a skilful way."

In addition to hotelier Roman Skoblo (Savoy Group), they were aided by a team including

architects Kadel Quick Scheib (construction), the Munich design studio Lemongras and designers Vogt + Weizenegger for interior decorating and furnishing. They created 171 rooms on a total of seven floors, in a way, which can be described as minimalist, pure, and any other Bauhaus adjective that comes to mind. This restraint and precision is also reflected in the furniture design. Every guest can relax for a length of time in the famous "Tongue" and "Series 7" chairs by Arne Jacobsen, because even the upper-class rooms are loft size. Of special interest: the TV rollers in a Fifties style by Lemongras. Inside these rolling cabinets in dark zebrano wood, the boob tube becomes a work of art, much more than just an appliance.

01 | Design classics characterise the
furnishings of Berlin's youngest design
hotel. In the foreground: a rolling TV
cart of dark zebrano wood in a 50's
style.

On each floor, there is only one colour in three different tones: dark blue, sky blue, light blue, or a bright yellow, sun yellow, and pastel yellow.

The lobby, divided into the reception, lounge, bar, and Internet workstation segments, is especially inviting. The flowing forms and colour harmonies of selected materials and lights are eye-catchers. The overall impression is decidedly posh, and yet the distinction of it all is that, whether it be vases, cups, lamps, furniture – all of it is made of inexpensive elements. A perfect environment for collecting good ideas – the proof: Good design does not have to be expensive.

02 | The reception area: minimalist, pure – but not cold.

03 | Small groups will also find space for conferences at Ku'damm 101.

04 | The lobby is cleverly divided into various segments. Here, a view of the lounge area.

05 | Jacobsen chairs in bright colours provide a contrast to the black and white areas.

06 | Pleasant sleep on comfortable mattresses in a calm atmosphere.

04

05 06

hopper st. antonius | cologne . germany

DESIGN: Rolf Kursawe

In close proximity to the centre of Cologne, which can be comfortably reached on foot, a second version of new hospitality was created within the walls of a building from the turn of the century. Since 1990 Jörn-Carsten Bube has been continuing the successful concept of the first Hopper Hotel, stressing the reduction of colours and shapes to enable an undisturbed dialogue between guests, space and art.

Constructed in 1904 as a brotherhood house for homeless men the building was dedicated to Saint Anthony the patron saint of the poor and wedded couples. Severely damaged during World War II and later rebuilt differently, it continued to serve the charity taking in the homeless, however as

demand for this kind of hostel continually decreased, the institution eventually closed in 1997. Together with the owner, Cologne architect Rolf Kursawe planned the building's redesign into a hotel. The old spirit was to be revived and the tradition of hospitality (if only for less needy guests) continued. Today one finds a sensitive juxtaposition of historical building material and contemporary design behind the façade of natural stone and brick. The original shape of the building was recreated to a large extent: one can once again admire the historic gabled stairs. Alterations that were necessary were undertaken with great sensitivity and respect for the history of the house. Soft colours, subtle materials and plain furniture create the suitable atmosphere for the

photography by contemporary artists, the presentation and advancement of which the Hopper Hotel St. Antonius has dedicated itself to.

39 rooms and 15 suites were created from the former sleeping and recreation rooms. The rooms are kept plain, the furniture is subtle, all reminiscent of the building's past. However, purist style does not mean sparse fittings: high quality materials replace cluttered detail. The furnishing is irresistibly plain and the subtle luxury can only be seen at second glance. Independent of whether one books a single room in the S category or one in XXL, the broad open atmosphere of the rooms has a pleasant and sophisticated effect. Kambala solid wooden

01 | The hotel has dedicated itself to the presentation and promotion of photography under the patronage of Professor L. Fritz Gruber.

hopper st. antonius | 95

02   03

parquet in red-brown tones, teak wood furniture with white upholstery and strict architectonic geometry lend the rooms a meditative calm.

Additionally, state-of-the-art technology, single kitchenettes in some of the suites and comfortable conference rooms make the hotel a relaxing place to work. The lobby, the bar and the Spitz restaurant are all situated on the ground floor. Vaulted ceilings and exposed Mettlach tiles of the former dining room allow the charm and hospitality of days gone by to be revived. Conforming to this, the tables and chairs are designed in only a moderately contemporary style. Different from the olden days, the menu today offers creative top dishes.

The inner courtyard modelled as a garden is an optical culinary delight: Holy Saint Anthony gazes at the goings on in the court. The historic statue is surrounded by terrace furniture inspired by Mediterranean influences, which sit on a finely raked gravel surface.

02 | The unique inner courtyard offers Mediterranean flair.

03 | The lobby: A former journeyman's hostel in a new context.

04 | Wonderfully suited to a relaxed business meeting: the Cathedral Suite.

05 | Minimalism with noble materials determines the design concept.

06 | A very exclusive goldfish pond.

04 05

06

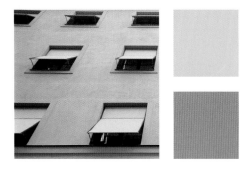

cortiina | munich . germany

DESIGN: Albert Weinzierl

Sleeping between Jurassic stone and bog oak? Bedded on natural rubber, wrapped in duvets made from untreated cotton? Sounds like hardcore camping in the wilderness. Yet, it is anything but that. In Munich's Hotel Cortiina, the wood, stone and fabrics come together in a modern way, radiating an air of natural nobility from every corner – subtle colours and straight lines that combine with natural plant and mineral substances to create a new ambience in the rooms. Not earthy, yet not artificial or overdone, but rather, elegant and, at the same time, clear-cut. Stylish living in the centre of the Bavarian state capital.

Rudi Kull and architect Albert Weinzierl, a well-known duo in the city who operate several trendy restaurants in Munich, launched the Cortiina in November of 2001. Their entrance into the luxury hotel business turned many heads – not least of all due to the establishment's name, which, at first glance looks like a typing error (and at second glance, too, for that matter). After extensive renovation work, the former Hotel Adler has been completely transformed: Once an aging address with a long-standing tradition, it is now an exclusive hotel with a New Edition look, in the middle of the historical city centre. Whether one is interested in theatre or museums, restaurants or luxury boutiques – the attractions in the city on the Isar are within the radius of a few minutes' walk.

Yet you can leave the noise and the bustle at the doorstep. The Cortiina is considered a "house of tranquillity", in which individualists can find relaxation and inspiration. A major contributor to this atmosphere is the design of the 33 rooms (between 22 and 30 square metres in size): parquet floors and panelling in warm oak, individually crafted furniture, with an open, clear layout and a glass wall along the bathroom side. In the bathroom, light natural stone tiles dominate. Chrome-plated aluminium basins and Vola fixtures provide a subtle touch. It is an environment which beckons guests to relax. One particular innovation developed by Cortiina together with an expert institute promises a special degree of comfort: the mattresses made of natural rubber, on which you can sleep like a baby.

The heart of the small design hotel is its lounge. In the morning, at the breakfast buffet, one can enjoy soft, classical music – or the sunshine in the green courtyard in summer. In the winter months, five-o'clock teas take place every weekend in the lobby. The tea tastes best at the open fireplace, finished in coarsely cut, grey Jura stone. Just picture it – sipping on mint tea by the flickering fire as dusk falls outside.

01 | Subtle colours, clear-cut shapes – a pleasant atmosphere in the centre of the city on the Isar.

cortiina I 99

02 03

04

02 | Lighting arrangement at the reception
     desk of the Munich design hotel.

03 | Cosy, yet not frumpy: the open fireplace
     made of coarsely cut natural stone in
     the lounge.

04 | Tailor-made view. The less voyeuristic
     guest can simply close the doors of the
     glass dividing wall.

05 | Discreet design and classical music at
     the breakfast table.

06 | In addition to cocktails, the bar also
     offers a small menu of exquisite wines.

07 | Subdued nobility: Natural materials and
     an open layout characterise the 33
     rooms of the Cortiina.

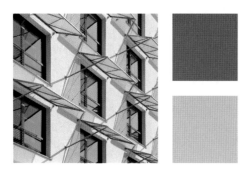

hotel josef | prague . czech republic

DESIGN: Eva Jiricna

"The Unbearable Lightness of Being" – if not before, then certainly after the publication of Milan Kundera's book, Prague rose to fame as the setting for a thoroughly modern narrative, adding another romantic refuge for the feeling of being alive today. Then came Philip Kaufman's fascinating cinematic interpretation starring Juliette Binoche and Daniel-Day Lewis. Amazing to think that, after the fall of the Iron Curtain, Prague has established itself as the Hollywood of the east, the setting for many great stories, with a young and vibrant social scene. Which means, cosmopolitans of the world, put Prague on your "must see" list.

People who appreciate the really beautiful things in life and have a kind of aesthetic sixth sense need to lay down their tender heads in a certain type of accommodation. Not always an easy matter in this metropolis on the River Vltava,

which – until now – has been a bit of a desert in that respect. But once Hotel Josef opened its doors in summer 2002, all that changed in one fell swoop. The first noteworthy design hotel in the Czech Republic, it is pointing the way for the rest of eastern Europe. From the outside, the hotel's appearance is light, transparent, youthful and relaxing – and even more so on the inside. Its steel and glass façade is like a pioneering new fragrance in the historical atmosphere of the old town, announcing the new style of architecture for the 21st century while managing to fit in with its surroundings. Guests only have to enter the hotel and walk across the bright reception area to find a lobby that immediately reveals the stylistic language of designer Eva Jiricna. It has a feminine feel with soft, tender forms, a palette of light, pastel tones and little decoration. A lucid "open space" from top to bottom. The spiral staircase is stunning; its glass steps give guests

the impression of floating – rather than moving – around the hotel. The same is true of the numerous guest rooms, which offer a striking quintessence of luxury and sophistication, with elegant Italian furniture and lacquered beds. Bathrooms are completely transparent and fantastically sexy – everything in them seems to be made of glass, except, of course, towels and soap. Eva Jiricna's style is already familiar to the fashion set. Originally from the Czech Republic, she has designed the Hugo Boss shops around the world.

Amid all the hustle and bustle of the city and the myriad shopping and sightseeing opportunities that Prague has to offer, Hotel Josef is an oasis of tasteful design. It has the hint of a shop feel about it, but it is quiet and very focused. Unbearably light stories of a Prague being, to which Hotel Josef is certain to become a regular contributor.

01 | The lobby with lounge and bar appeals with its light, bright nature.

02 03

04

05 06

07

02 | View from outside into the lounge.
A nightly meeting spot for the
cosmopolitan nightlife scene.

03 | Glass is the dominant material in the
bathrooms.

04 | The hotel possesses the only backyard
garden in Prague's historical city
centre. In the summer, it is an ideal
location for parties.

05 | Expressive colours and Italian furniture
in the rooms.

06 | Stairway to Heaven. A glass winding
staircase leads up to the lobby.

07 | Showering in the middle of the room.
The glass shower stalls let no water out,
but allow peeks inside.

das triest | vienna . austria

DESIGN : Peter Lorenz, James Soane (CD Partnership)

With the opening of Das Triest in 1995, Vienna finally had its own hip hotel centrepiece – a sharp contrast from the city's charming, late 19th-century, art nouveau architecture. History, however, shows the Das Triest to actually have some humble beginnings. A former coach station on the route from Vienna to Trieste, the building was wasting away, operating as a simple inn before its owners decided to convert the site into a unique and contemporary five-star hotel.

The property's renovation contract was awarded to the Innsbruck-based architect Peter Lorenz, whose eventual design foreshadowed an on-going separation between the old and the new. Over the fourth floor, Lorenz set up a prominent,

sheet metal-lined structure with an "attic" roof appearance. This structural intervention created new space which not only allowed for luxurious rooms and views, but also gave the building much needed modernity. For the interior architecture, the hotel's developers chose to rely on an established design approach and partnered with London-based Sir Terence Conran. The resulting architecture, while at times converging stylistically, nonetheless results in an overall unity which is eagerly inviting.

The Das Triest's interior boasts a pleasant appearance, one which may at first appear less Austrian than other Lorenz designs, but still contains the high levels of craftsmanship.

Interior architect James Soane underlines his love of detail through his charmingly tailored selection of furniture materials – namely cherry wood – which suits the demands of a luxury lifestyle hotel in the centre of the city. The hotel's 60 rooms quickly convey to guests a sense of Viennese flair through their lovely design. In particular, the penthouse Triest suite and its wrap-around 160 square metre terrace, make an imposing photographic backdrop. Meanwhile, the Triest's 12 other suites are so popular that they are passed around from confidant to confidant within an ever-widening circle of design hotel enthusiasts. So even if money is no object, securing a reservation at the Das Triest may very well be.

01 | The best drinks in Vienna are mixed at
the "Silver Bar" of the Triest.

02 | The architecture is a harmonious interplay of old and new.

03 | Adjacent room to the lobby with view of the garden courtyard. The arches are reminiscent of the former horse carriage station.

04 | It has been providing heat since the Imperial Age: the open fireplace in the lobby.

05 | An impressive staircase links the six floors of the hotel.

06 | A cross-section shows the arrangement of the guest rooms and penthouse.

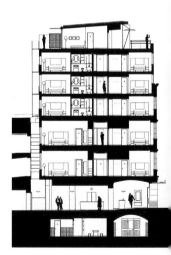

07 | Vienna lifestyle. The rooms are
primarily adorned in warm colours.

08 | From the roof terrace of the Triest Suite
in the penthouse, guests have a glorious
view of the city.

augarten hotel | graz . austria
DESIGN: Günter Domenig

The Augarten Hotel in Graz is testament to the Austrian town's immense cultural heritage. Combining culture and art with a beautiful place to stay, this building is far from what is generally associated with Austrian guesthouses. Don't come in the hope of finding carved balcony railings and window shutters with small hearts or overhanging chandeliers and heavy carpets. Instead prepare for more refined, contemporary spaces, with designer furniture and art in abundance. Artwork is prominent, particularly in the public areas. It also features largely in the rooms and holiday apartments. A stay becomes a cultural pleasure with work by Gunter Damisch, Martin Kippenberger, Hans Staudacher, Elke Krystufek, Matta Wagnest and Rudi Molacek, amongst others.

The four-star hotel designed by Günther Domenig is in a quiet but central location, in easy walking distance to the old part of Graz. In addition to the well established Schlossberg Hotel this is the second project by Helmut Marko in which he delivers an individualised, culturally oriented hotel concept. The hotel has 36 rooms and 20 holiday apartments. All are generously sized and practically equipped, with furniture from notable design houses including Cappellini and Ligne Roset. Extensive windows, white walls and wooden floors ensure a bright, casual atmosphere, with most rooms sporting south-facing balconies or terraces to create additional space. Technology has not been overlooked either. All of the necessary modem and fax connections for a mobile office are at hand in each room. The holiday apartments are between 35 and 70 square metres in size and are furnished with everything that is required for a mid- to long-term stay. This includes a fully-equipped kitchen with a cooker, microwave, and

refrigerator, as well as cutlery and cooking utensils. Each apartment has a living room with comfortable seating just off the bedroom.

There is an in-house "wellness" area with a swimming pool that allows at least eight strong breaststrokes. If a jogging session along the Mur River does not appeal, guests can opt for some exertion in the gym, and then take a sauna and solarium. The chill-out area is a fabulous finale to any exercise regime encouraging relaxation and calm. Just as relaxing is the view of the Graz clock tower and surrounds from the hotel's roof terrace. From a business perspective, the Augarten Hotel has a great deal more to offer than a place to stay and relax in. It is also very well equipped for professional training sessions, workshops and seminars. The two meeting rooms, both between 37 and 38 square metres, seat approx. 20 people.

01 | The apartments shine with a room size of up to 70 square metres and their objective, aesthetic interior décor.

augarten hotel | 111

02 03
04 05

02 | In the restaurant, chef Johann Mayer specialises in light cuisine
with Western and Eastern accents.

03 | In the studio-like apartments, guests will also find fully equipped
kitchens.

04 | Artificial floor lamps in the apartments.

05 | White plastered walls and large windows provide brightness and
stand in harmonious contrast to the warm wooden floor and
colourful upholstered furniture.

06 | Seating arrangement in the lobby.

07 | Swimming pool, sauna, fitness equipment and a steam bath in
the wellness area provide relaxation. The glass façade can be slid
back and forth.

greulich | zurich . switzerland

DESIGN: Romero & Schaefle, Jean Pfaff

"Guess who was at the Greulich the other day…" is likely be the opening gambit in many an excited conversation in the near and more distant future. Despite being a cosmopolitan city and Switzerland's biggest, Zurich also has something villagey about it. News travels fast, with haunts favored by people who like seeing and being seen soon becoming the talk of the town. One example is this recently opened contemporary hotel not far from the station. It has a bar and a restaurant and everything it takes to appeal to a certain section of Zurich society.

But why, you may ask, the name "Greulich" (meaning "greyish" or "awful" in German)? An element of understatement is at work here, giving the property – the essence of style, through and through – a brand image running counter to reality. Actually, the reasons are quite simple. The hotel is on the corner where Stauffacher

Strasse meets Herman Greulich Strasse. And, because Herman Greulich was one of the forefathers of Switzerland's union and class struggle movement, the name still has overtones of social revolution.

Not that this is really an issue here. The hotel's image - completely in keeping with a young, sophisticated lifestyle – satisfies all the aesthetic requirements of good design, with plenty of voguish art to entertain the eye. The slightly curved façade is a retro touch of Werkbund modernism; its ground-floor window frontage allows passers-by to look straight in on the activity in the bar and restaurant. Even here, the design has a sense of formal rigor – Zen meditation, even – that is continued throughout the 10 garden rooms and 8 junior suites. Although the effect might seem a touch chilly and radically minimalistic, it sets off artist Jean

Pfaff's subtle color palette to perfection. Besides, it is a nod towards to the building's past as a former workshop and also creates a great ambience for drinks at the hotel's public bar. Here, guests raise their glasses and comment, in surprise: the hotel even has a garden out the back! Another tour de force of intense concentration: a birch grove in a gravel bed, a strictly rhythmical arrangement.

And, as visual pleasures need cuisine to match, 'slow food' is very much the order of the day at the hotel's restaurant. Catalan chef David Martinez Salvany serves up traditional dishes and new trends that bear the signature of his Mediterranean roots. Matters of taste, just like the dominance of the design at the Greulich, whose aura is hard to resist. For one thing, it makes for a very good opening line: "Guess who was at the Greulich the other day…".

01 | Simple, and simply beautiful.
The rooms have a radically reduced
feeling and exude pure tranquillity.

02 03
04

02 | The slightly curved façade is
   reminiscent of Werkbund architecture.

03 | Wide ramps lead from the courtyard to
   the rooms.

04 | In Restaurant Greulich – corresponding
   to the architecture – high-class cuisine
   is served.

05 | The birch grove in the backyard invites
   guests to meditate.

06 | You can work well here. There is
   nothing to distract you from what is
   essential.

07 | The sleek forms and functional design
   can be found in the bathrooms as well.

widder hotel | zurich . switzerland

DESIGN: Tilla Theus

If it weren't just a few steps from the infamous Bahnhofstrasse in central Zurich, the Hotel Widder would almost be a hamlet of a hotel. Ten historical former residences – many dating back to the Middle Ages – have been joined together to create an unusual Swiss hotel collaboration. Forty-two rooms and seven suites have emerged from this charming, luxurious labyrinth of a hotel – a hotel that many proclaim the best in all of Switzerland. Although it may appear a physical impossibility, the Widder's mathematics mean that a mere 4.9 rooms exist per building, a theoretical rather than literal deconstruction of the hotel, but one which nonetheless gives an idea of the generous approach taken by the Widder's backers, the Swiss Banking Society. It's not just the size of the rooms that imparts a feeling of urban living within the hotel, it's the sensitive architecture by Tilla Theus as well. Theus has created within the Widder a sovereign

microcosm that seamlessly links historical materials with present day structural processes along with construction methods, sharp details and an innovative sense of design. By subtly intermingling single buildings via staircases, porticos and inner courtyards, a feeling of intimacy and exclusive security has been created in the hotel's public spaces. These include the Widder Restaurant, the Turmstubli or Tower Bar, the Wirtschaft zum Schtund, the hotel's magical garden, and the Widder Bar. This is clearly an atmosphere of exclusivity. Should one encounter a person of public prestige, discretion and respectful distance is expected. Nonetheless, the Widder is also a place where such persons are likely to engage in conversation with friends and strangers alike, thanks to its relaxed, yet refined atmosphere. Nowhere is this spirit more embodied than in one of the top-floor suites, which boast rooftop terraces that offer

spectacular city views, a perfect respite on warm summer nights. A ride in a Widder elevator is a must for the visitor. The filigree lattice cages rattle along through the hotel's old walls of square, unadorned stone. Here, modern technology and historical construction meet directly and impressively. For those interested solely in an architectural study, the Widder alone is worth a trip to Zurich. Its masonry joints, corner connections, door and window casings and wall and ceiling moldings are but a few of the Widder's rich examples of masterful, architectural detail. These clearly evoke stylistic shadows of other prominent architects, while boasting their own unique features. Thus, the Widder – like the Casello in Verona by Carlo Scarpa or the Museum in the Castello Montebello by Campi, Pessina and Piazzoli in Bellinzona – is recommended for travellers with a keen appreciation of style, design and luxury.

01 | The Widder Bar. An insider tip, for more than just jazz fans. Zurich's exclusive socialites gather here.

02 | 03

02 | Classic furniture with a clear design harmonizes well with the historical rooms.

03 | Two storey living room, bedroom and working area in room number 509 in the "Haus zum Bankknecht".

04 | Filigree steel scaffolding with staircase and elevator meets the brick and roughcast walls.

05 | The morning espresso tastes even better under the large glass roof.

06 | Roof top terrace with a view. In the background lies the Lake Zurich.

07 | The restored stairwell is supported by elements of the original.

08 | Outlines of the buildings spread over Widdergasse, Augustinergasse and Rennweg.

04 05

06

08

07

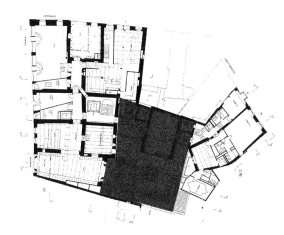

the hotel | lucerne . switzerland

DESIGN: Jean Nouvel

Popular with a young, hip and international crowd, The Hotel has a 25-room boutique style that breaks the luxurious 5-star Swiss mould. This is Switzerland's first non-branded, urban luxury hotel, situated in an abundant park setting in the heart of Lucerne. It is the collaboration of French architect extraordinaire Jean Nouvel, responsible for Lucerne's impressive Culture and Convention Centre that is now a city landmark, and Hotelier Urs Karli.

The Hotel, formerly an art nouveau town house, has been transformed into a super-slick, ultra-modern oasis of hospitality. Guests are not there merely to sleep and eat, but also to be entertained. This forward-thinking approach has been achieved

by creating interesting spaces that form a backdrop for people watching, where passers-by become part of the performance. Scenes from the architect's favourite films are projected onto ceilings to stimulate interactivity, adding to the excitement and magic. These are illuminated at night providing an extraordinary 'moving mosaic' when viewed from the outside.

A key concept of the hotel's design was to remove divisions between outside and inside. This has been cleverly achieved, giving people outside the impression they are in and those inside that they are out. Ground floor and basement barriers have also been eliminated by the architect's skilful interplay of mirrors. The juxtaposition creates a

feeling that the lobby is floating above the restaurant.

The rooms themselves could be interpreted as theatre. Again, film clips are shown overhead and each has its own colour scheme, all in soothing tones offering a sense of calm and tranquillity alongside the silent, moving images. A mix of materials has been used with an interesting interpretation of linear elements. All horizontal panels are made of wood and all vertical panels made of stainless steel. Custom designed furniture including desks, beds, armchairs and side tables have the Jean Nouvelle hallmark. Every room has large windows with dramatic views of the city and the park. The suites have

01 | Each of the 25 rooms has a scene from
a well-known movie projected on the
ceiling. Room 5201 plays 'Matador'
from Spanish director Pedro Almodovar.

02 03

a patio and continue the fascinating interplay of interior and exterior spaces. Bathrooms ooze sex appeal and overlook a private outdoor area planted with bamboo and exotic plants, simulating an outdoor shower experience in the tropics. Guests and visitors can enjoy the restaurant Bam Bou, where chef Andrew Clayton has created a stunning mix of traditional French cuisine infused with Asian influences.

The space itself is impressive, again displaying a sophisticated use of mirrors to reverse the order of interior and exterior. This is certainly one of Lucerne's most stylish restaurants. The Lounge – a drinking haven alongside the restaurant – is as much a social hub of the hotel as the lobby.

Guests can relax in comfortable armchairs, continue to be entertained by the surrounding environment and enjoy the 'soul' of the place. It is also a popular spot for locals who want to get a piece of the action.

The Hotel is a destination for the well travelled; those who base their decisions on lifestyle and experiences, who demand style, comfort and service, and most of all appreciate design excellence.

02 | A view into "The Lounge" Bar.

03 | At the Bam-Bou Restaurant, top exotic French cuisine is served.

04 | The Lounge bar – a stylish destination for guests and locals.

05 | The super-slick lobby area with visual installations for colour and entertainment.

06 | The chrome and wood furniture was designed by Jean Nouvel especially for the hotel.

07 | A movie scene from Frederico Fellini's 'Casanova' in the Garden Park Deluxe Suite.

04 05
06 07

hotel greif | bolzano . italy

DESIGN: Boris Podrecca

Swathed in history dating back to the Middle Ages, the reincarnation of Bolzano's Hotel Greif was not one of refurbishment alone. An entire project encompassing restoration, new construction, urban improvement and landscaping has transformed a very old building and a fine urban area into a multifunctional city centre that brings the South Tyrol capital alive. There are still links to the ancient Black Griffin Inn, as the hotel was originally known. Historians have traced its beginnings back to 1600. Today, the new hotel has been built on the centuries-old foundation walls and a passage linking Walther Square and Via della Rena has created a new piazzetta, reminiscent of days of old.

Viennese architect Boris Podrecca was responsible for the perfect symbiosis of traditional and contemporary architecture that is the very core of the hotel. The project as a whole is a successful marriage of old and new. An imposing glass and steel structure, that is now the entrance to the hotel, frames huge antique wooden doors. The theme flows through to the interiors, with traditional terrazzo floors alongside contemporary finishes such as local Maplewood in the reception area. Rooms have been furnished using a combination of antique 'Biedermeier' pieces that belonged to the former hotel and new designs by the architect that were made in the hotel's own carpentry shop over the duration of the refurbishment.

Each room has an individually commissioned contemporary artwork. Owner Franz Staffler selected a number of contemporary artists to create an individual piece for all 33 rooms. Each artist was assigned a room and asked to furnish it with his or her artwork. In some cases, the modern art has been combined with a less recent piece, reaffirming the juxtaposition of old and new. It is not only the artwork that brings individuality to every room. Furnishings and configurations are also unique, with extensive use of natural materials including silk fabrics, wool carpet and oiled wooden floors. A different kind of marble has been used in every bathroom. Of course the appeal goes beyond the aesthetic. Beds are extra long and each room is equipped with a laptop and internet access. For those of musical persuasion, the room with the fully restored Blüthner grand piano must be requested.

Bolzano's Hotel Greif is a gallery of sorts, both in terms of the art collection and the cleverly sculptured structure itself. It should see lovers of contemporary art returning thirty three times over, just to experience every room and admire the individual works in each.

01 | Modern interior decorating in a historical building. The staircase in the Duplex Suite.

02 | A suite containing a piano is available for musical guests.

03 | Asian-inspired screens and dark wenge parquet – anything but ordinary in this Southern Tyrolean metropolis.

04 | The heavy wooden door is a historical treasure in the foyer.

05 | The design of the rooms and suites is modern, yet not a bit cold.

06 | A look in the lobby, with reception area and extraordinary seating.

07 | Biedermeier and modern meet in the lounge as well.

the gray | milan . italy

DESIGN: Guido Ciompi

An ultra-smart new lifestyle hotel just dropped into Milan's fashion district around Via Monte-napoleone and Via Spiga. The Gray, Milan's newest design hotel, opened its doors in summer 2003 right in the heart of Italy's design capital – on quiet Via San Raffaele by a side entrance to the Galleria Vittorio Emannuele. The Gray occupies a double five-storey building – a former residence with elaborate late 19th-century façade and a seamlessly adjoining former 1960s office building with sober stone frontage. From the outside, nothing suggests hotel activity here, but cast your eyes into the bar and lobby and the hotel's signature design concept is instantly revealed.

Suspended from the ceiling is a red-velvet covered divan, swaying like a sedan chair above reception, which – like the walls, the ceiling and the full-length drapes – has a new color mood every few minutes. A computer-generated show of hundreds of tiny lights bathes the lobby and its expanses of black flagstones in blue; the next, in tones of green, pink or red. Even the collection of spirits in "Il Bar" – separated only by a sliding glass panel and curtain – is constantly changing its look as one lighting effect flows into another.

The hotel concept and design are by Florentine architect and designer Guido Ciompi, who made his name with designs for Gucci boutiques and private villas. His stylistic hallmark is a muted formal language using clear, geometric lines. Ciompi's rooms are fairly purist but include experimental surfaces (rippled plaster, top dyeing techniques, gilding etc.), unusual material collages and ethnic accessories. The result is an individual style, a clever balancing act between opulence and elegance. Though some details nod towards fashion, the architecture as a whole appears timeless and has all the promise of becoming a modern classic. The different layouts of the 21 guest rooms were Ciompi's cue for designing each one in its own individual style. The choice ranges from a compact corner room to bi-level duplex suites with filigree steel staircases or a suite with its own gym. Bathrooms are especially generous in size and design. Some rooms have their own steamroom, others a circular jacuzzi with TV screens around the side.

Guests also have the choice of a room with a wooden or a carpeted floor. Some are bright white or in neutral shades of beige; earthy tones predominate in others. All rooms, however, share the same interior fittings that were custom-designed for The Gray: sleek, craftsman-finished fitted closets of limed wood, colored room partitions, tables of Makassar ebony, integrated ash paneling for walls and beds, leather upholstery and ethnic African artifacts and accessories.

01 | The lobby, finished in large, black stone
slabs, is computer controlled, and
continually bathed in a new light.

05

06

02 | An eye-opener in the lobby. A reddish-
purple divan hangs from the ceiling.

03 | Restaurant with furniture in clear
geometrical lines.

04 | Each room is individually designed.

05 | The collection of spirits in the hotel bar
"Il Bar" is also regularly bathed in a
different light.

06 | In the Duplex Suite, a futuristic steel
staircase leads to the sleeping area.

delle arti design hotel | cremona . italy

DESIGN: Giorgio Palù, Michele Bianchi

Thanks to Antonio Stradivari, Cremona is well known among violinists. Amid the medieval scenery, the hyper-modern Dellearti opened its doors in 2002 – and its name says it all. It is not only artistically decorated, but also a fitting venue for art exhibits and music events. This building, in which glass is the dominant material, is a prominent eye-catcher in its environment, which is characterised by Renaissance structures. On the spot upon which the hotel is located once stood the Monte di Pietà, as the city's pawnshop was called. Architects Giorgio Palù and Michele Bianchi have reflected exactly the style of that former "Merciful Mountain" in the hotel's façade: The foyer is adorned with two outsize columns made of anthracite-coloured stone blocks. However, the heavy impression of bulk and mass of these columns quickly disappears when one focuses on the glass panels situated to the left and right. Speaking

of glass: Palù and Bianchi selected it, along with steel and wenge wood, as the dominant materials. Thus, the façade glows blue and golden every evening, generating the impression of delicacy and transparency.

The hotel lobby also has an air of modern purism: Le Corbusier tables and sofas greet guests in a space equipped with high ceilings. A narrow walkway made of glass and polished metal leads to an open gallery with a computer work area, games and a small library. Monitors built flush into the walls provide a non-stop look at the flickering world of Italian video artists. The light well to the right of the video wall offers a place to exhibit works of contemporary artists. Thirty double rooms, two suites and one apartment with kitchenette, spread over three floors, are grouped around the courtyard. The rooms have similar furnishings, but with different details,

although all reflect the designers' notion of exclusive functionalism. Instead of night tables, guests will find rolling marble slab carts; a shelf that seems to float in mid-air harbours a television and serves double duty as a desk.

Hotel director Emilio Sacchi and his team cater especially to a younger clientele of business travellers: The rooms are equipped with Internet, fax and voicemail capability. The design bar serves appetizers and small Italian snacks. Yet the staff can also arrange dinner events in the medieval Breda de Bugni castle, as well as hiking and bicycle trips along the Po River. Guests can also keep fit in the hotel's own fitness room. Those preferring to relax can enjoy the steam bath, Jacuzzi and sauna.

01 | A different kind of hotel hallway. The curved wall with an elegant look is reminiscent of a large, heavy curtain.

02 03

04

05 | 06

02 | 03 The 33 rooms and suites are
grouped around a courtyard. Video art
by Italian artists is projected on the
opposite walls.

04 | Reception area with steel appeal.

05 | The tables in the breakfast room, made
of wenge wood, were designed
especially for the hotel.

06 | Steel and glass are the dominating
materials.

continentale | florence . italy

DESIGN: Michele Bonan

A pageboy haircut with a jade piercing, a smile that swishes by. Then, two dark-haired beauties come into view, chatting and strolling down the bridge. Glimpses from the Ponte Vecchio – projected on a screen in the foyer showing live images from the nearby streets and piazzas. People checking into the Hotel Continentale find themselves already in the midst of the action – literally. This hotel with a savvy sense of lifestyle that opened in January of 2003 is located in the heart of Florence, just a few steps away from the famous palazzi of the Medici era.

The Continentale is the latest project of the compact but competent Lungarno Group, which is part of fashion designer Salvatore Ferragamo's empire. In the Tuscan capital alone, the Group maintains three further luxury hotels, each with its own individual character. The Continentale adds a new face to this constellation – the atmosphere of "contemporary pleasing": An atmosphere in which inspiration and enjoyment are fused. Interior decorator Michele Bonan has used the Italian style of the 50's for his orientation, a style that includes la dolce vita as well as neo-realism from the likes of Vittorio de Sica or provocation à la Pasoloni. Instead of an excess of retro elements, he has created a meeting place for the new nomads, where a joie de vivre and the art of life of the past decade have been translated into the present, using clear, light rooms, selected details, and usual arrangements.

It all begins in the entryway. A work by artist Fabrizio Corneli greets newcomers, an installation named "Strain", which has an unusual effect amid the comings and goings of guests. The area of tension that develops stretches across the entire foyer, from the video scenes at the reception desk to the non-cushy, minimal fireplace niche, and is characteristic for the Continentale – a blend of stimulation and a sense of well-being, reflected in the 43 rooms. The rooms, several with terrace access, offer a panoramic view of the sea of red-tiled roofs and the Arno River, which snakes through the city. The interior strikes a balance between high-tech and soft design. White veils that catch the Tuscan sunlight billow around the sleeping areas, and replicas of 50's

01 | The play of Tuscan sunlight: This is how the new nomads of the international jet set sleep.

era lamps are scattered throughout the rooms that are decorated with furniture communicating unadorned elegance. In addition, a penthouse suite is available for special wishes, as well as the "Terrazza dei Consorti" Sky Lounge: by day, a quiet little place to catch some rays, by night the ideal spot to meet over drinks.

Guests of the Continentale will find relaxation in the hotel's wellness centre, including sauna and massage. Or they can stretch out in the easy chairs of the reading room and enjoy the panorama of the Ponte Vecchio. Those more in the mood for entertainment will enjoy exploring the Home Theatre Lounge, where one will find the newest generation in visual entertainment.

And afterwards? We recommend ending the day in the Lounge Bar, which is also open to the public. Face to face with the cream of Florentine society, you can enjoy a finely distilled grappa – and plunge into the feeling of "contemporary pleasing".

02 | Simple elegance and billowing fabric: The interior translates the Italian style of the 50's into the here and now.

03 | A love for detail.

04 | Relaxing in style in one of the 43 rooms of the Continentale.

05 | Not cramped, not confining: Light, unadorned design in the bathroom.

06 | Clear forms, right down to the details.

05 06

gallery hotel art | florence . italy

DESIGN: Michele Bonan

While Florence has long been known as a destination for art and art-lovers, travellers with a penchant for contemporary design, modern furnishings and a chic appreciation for discretion have lacked a hotel to call their own. So it's no surprise that when such a hotel finally opened its doors in May 1999 it was the brainchild not of hotel developers, but of fashion designers – and not just any fashion house at that. Perched on the Arno's north bank within steps of the Ponte Vecchio, the Gallery Hotel Art is a 56-room hotel, stylishly and sleekly opened by the Ferragamo family and designed by architect Michele Bonan. Like other "art"-themed hotels in Berlin, Barcelona and Glasgow, the Gallery Hotel Art has created

an environment in which art and accommodation work in tandem to edify the guest experience both in-house and out. With its fashionable pinstriped rooms, black-and-white images of Florentine landmarks and Japanese-styled sliding screen doors, this is the hotel intrepid Italia-philes have long been waiting for.

While the Gallery Hotel has strived to create a contemporary feel, its attention to detail and authenticity is resolutely Old World. In keeping with Florence's tradition as an Anglophone haven, for example, the hotel's library stocks first editions of English literature classics on subjects ranging from cinema to fashion to art, handpicked for

their singular and collective value. Along with a dominant, dual-chromatic colour scheme, the rooms contain uniquely designed furnishings such as pigskin and wenge armchairs, as well as abundant natural lighting through horizontally panelled windows.

In the lobby, Bonan and the Ferragamos have chosen to head east, introducing Oriental elements such as Burmese lacquered objects d'art – more typical of a Buddhist temple than a city best known for its Christian Duomo. Such ancient designs are then balanced with images of high 20th-century modernism: Original Alberto Reggianini insect paintings in a taupe-and-grey

01 | Relaxing or dining above the roofs of the Renaissance city. In the background the tower of the famous Pallazzio Vecchio.

02 03   04

corner of the lobby area. This initial reception
area flows forward toward a rear 15th-century
courtyard containing original Renaissance
columns. Art, fashion and history are the
consummate Italian troika – all of which
converge at the Gallery Hotel Art. It's a mix that
might stun hotel purists. But the shock of the
new is always initially unsettling.

02 | Duplex Suite with an exclusive spot for
      sightseeing.

03 | The reduced design opens the eye to
      detail.

04 | The hotel hosts changing art and photo
      exhibitions in its public rooms.

05 | 06 The combination of black wood and
      pastel-coloured fabrics creates a
      timelessly elegant atmosphere.

07 | Art is the central theme – and avid
      readers will always find an interesting
      book to page through.

05 06

07

ca' pisani | venice . italy

DESIGN: Roberto Luigi Canovaro, Pierluigi Pescolderung

The first design hotel in Venice and a completely new concept in Venetian accommodation, Ca' Pisani is located close to the San Marco area in the peaceful district of Accademia. Owned by the Serandrei family, the hotel pays tribute to both historic grandeur and progress. It successfully maintains Italian heritage whilst at the same time reflects the brothers' passion for artistic forms of the Futuristic period.

Many characteristics of the original building, formerly a Venetian residence, are still intact and great care was taken to ensure that both the façade and the shell were restored to original condition. Walls have been treated the classic Italian way using special painting techniques and soft hues of mustard yellow and terracotta. Exposed timber beams, grand marble archways and ornate doorway mouldings all salute its former glory and have been cleverly integrated

with rather unexpected interiors. The new design of the 29-room hotel is a blend of avant-garde trends that emerged between the two World Wars. The lobby is inspired by the essential elements of Futurism – geometric shapes furnish the walls and etched glass and mirrors are a dominant feature. Futurist materials, including 'starlight' – an innovative material creating the effect of hundreds of small shining stars – have been used extensively.

The rooms are authentically furnished with 1930s and 1940s originals, in finishes of chrome, black leather and walnut wood that defined the era. Bedlinens are stylish and contemporary and boast a colour palette of caramel, cream and chocolate. Parquet flooring has been used throughout, some patterned in contrasting shades of timber. The hotel's wine and cheese bar 'La Rivista', whose namesake is that of an

original 1925 flower design by Futuristic artist Fortunato Depero, is a lively and extravagant cafe. Other designs by the same artist decorate the space, and are from the owners' private collection.

The roof terrace has more to offer than a spectacular vision of ancient domes, steeples and terracotta tiles. It is also the location of the Turkish bath that is available to guests, another unexpected addition to the eclectic style of this hotel.

01 | There is no Venetian kitsch here. In the rooms, you will find futuristic new interpretations of the styles of the 30's and 40's.

02 03

04

148 | ca' pisani

02 | Mosaic-like floor covering in the hallway connecting the rooms.

03 | 04 The stairs in the former palazzo are sometimes rustic, and sometimes futuristically transparent.

05 | The surfaces of the baths shimmer like thousands of little stars.

06 | Romantic spot to relax under palm trees – in a classically modern atmosphere.

07 | Walnut wood, patterned marble floors and colourful walls in the foyer.

08 | Befitting the furniture, art lovers will find pieces from the phase of Italian futurism.

ca' pisani | 149

hotel art | rome . italy

DESIGN: Raniero Botti, Gianfranco Mangiarotti

Via Margutta is one of the many surprises that are scattered throughout Rome. Just when you've left the crowds behind at the Spanish Steps, you turn one corner and arrive in a small, narrow lane with low, cotto coloured buildings that one might also find in a small Italian town. This unique atmosphere of the Via Margutta has always attracted artists. Gallerists and antique dealers followed, and, most recently, fashion designers such as Gucci and Valentino. With the opening of the Hotel Art in the rooms of a former college in the spring of 2003, this picturesque street has now definitively become chic.

Just one look at the long, narrow side stairs leading to the reception area, the walls shimmering in white marble, the floor, plastered with tiny white pebbles, and, on the wall, the magnificent lighting system designed by Enzo Catellani, stirs one's expectations: As if sitting in cracked-open eggshells formed out of the synthetic material used for boats, the receptionist and concierge sit and view the hotel lobby, which formerly served as a chapel. Its cross vaults were meticulously restored, and the ceiling painted in its original blue and dotted with countless small halogen lamps. Together with the giant lamps resembling clouds by Catellani, you might get the impression that you are standing under a starry sky. The Venetian marble floor, modelled after that in the Pantheon, underscores the splendour of the setting. Upon the aubergine-coloured tables, curved like birds' wings, in the lobby's bar and restaurant, a sumptuous breakfast is served, with fresh fruit and lusciously smelling dolcis that literally melt in your mouth.

Light and colour are the two central themes of the design concept. The hallways were decorated in shocking hues reminiscent of the Sixties: grass green, orange, yellow and cobalt blue. Light strips on the floor with lines of poetry by García Lorca and Octavio Paz lead the way to the 46 rooms. The rooms themselves, with their wenge wood floors, are more subdued. High-quality materials were used for their décor. The leather headboards on the beds are handmade, and the comfortable mattresses hold the promise of restful sleep.

01 | Light and colour as the central themes:
The silver fountain bowls by Paolo Giotti
gently light the passage to the lobby,
with its original cross vaulting.

02

03

02 | It is impossible to miss your floor: each of the four floors is
decorated in a different, vivid colour. The glass covering the walls
and floors lends a transparent character to the hallways.

03 | The concierge's workplace has a futuristic look.

04 | Contemporary works of art serve as an exciting contrast to the
historical building structure.

05 | 06 Light strips on the floors with lines of poetry by Octavio Paz
lead the way to the rooms.

07 | All 46 rooms are furnished with the latest technological
equipment, such as cordless notebooks for surfing the web.

bentley hotel | istanbul . turkey

DESIGN: Piero Lissoni, Nicoletta Canesi

Welcome to the European part of town: modern, elegant Istanbul, where the contrasts between Armani and ayram (the local yogurt drink), Boss and the bazaars, Living Divani and divans (traditional Turkish style) are particularly strong. This is where Istanbul's emergent social set gets together to see and be seen, oozing cosmopolitan self-assurance and panache. The Bentley Hotel is one of Istanbul's most sought-after addresses for today's business traveler as well as for the city's young socialites.

Located high above the city, it is a tall, slender building whose anthracite-colored façade blends into the cityscape with studied discretion. The two penthouse suites offer fabulous views of the center of Istanbul, the Bosphorus and the Golden Horn, with terraces spacious enough to accommodate a private outdoor shower. For the Bentley Hotel, Milanese designer Piero Lissoni

has used glass, light and olive-colored wood to tastefully reflect authentic elements of Turkish style. In the spirit of true Italian design, he avoids all skittishness and allows clear-cut forms, lines and colors to create an aesthetic oasis which is easy on the eye after the visual feast that is Istanbul. Floor-to-ceiling windows and understated wall colors – pale tones of beige, gray and green – produce a feeling of transparency and light in the hotel's rooms and suites. Glazing accounts for more than half of the wall space in the "corner rooms". Piero Lissoni has allowed himself one single curved stylistic feature in the whole hotel: a gleaming white staircase that winds itself round an elliptical column – the backbone, as it were, pure and unadorned, of the tall, slender building.

The contrast between the hotel's interior and the outside world – cool elegance juxtaposed with

the buzz of the Istanbul bazaars – is most palpable in the bar and restaurant. The bar is an uncomplicated interpretation of a Turkish café, with comfortable easy chairs and long rows of sofas with upholstery fabrics suggestive of Oriental designs. Lissoni has placed an illuminated wall of turquoise glass behind the bar, making a surprisingly strong color statement in the palette of the hotel's public spaces with their otherwise muted colors.

Elsewhere, color is allowed to "seep" into the rooms of the Bentley Hotel from outside. Looking through the glass front of the lobby is like seeing the lights on busy Halaskargazi Street flickering on a cinema screen while remaining detached from the activity outdoors. An even more intense experience of this perspective is to be had through the glass front of the mezzanine restaurant, which floats freely above the lobby

01 | The floor-to-ceiling windows lend the rooms a light and airy atmosphere.

bentley hotel | 155

02 03

04

and the hotel entrance and has a choice of modern fusion cuisine based on Turkish dishes with strong French and Italian influences. Though the restaurant atmosphere is almost austere overall, Lissoni allows himself one elaborate gesture within the crisp lines and starkly contrasting pale leather and dark wood: hanging above a single round table is a crystal chandelier, a final touch of mystery.

05

06

02 | A magnificent view of the centre of the city on the Bosporus unfolds from both roof suites.

03 | 04 Furnishings in the rooms and bathrooms are characterised by clear lines.

05 | The colour scheme is kept purposefully neutral. The colourful life outside shines in the window.

06 | The bar is an emphatically simple, new interpretation of a Turkish café.

hotel summary

Country / Location		Address	Information	Architecture & Design	Page
Spain	Palma de Mallorca	Portixol	opened 1999	Rafael Vidal	8
		Calle Sirena 27	23 rooms, 11 with terraces	Christian Aronsen	
		07006 Palma de Mallorca	conference and meeting facilities	Johanna Landström	
		España	restaurant, cocktail bar with terrace	Mikael Landström	
			outdoor pool with sun terrace and shade deck		
		www.portixol.com	located just outside the city centre		
Spain	Barcelona	Hotel Claris	built 1892, reopened 1991	Josep Martorell	12
		Pau Claris 150	124 guestrooms including 20 junior suites,14 duplex suites,	Oriol Bohigas	
		08009 Barcelona	4 large suites, 5 meeting rooms for up to 150 people	David Mackay	
		España	gym, sauna and roof-top swimming pool	MBM Architects	
			Catalan cuisine, terrace restaurant		
		www.hotelclaris.com	located in the centre of Barcelona		
Spain	Barcelona	Prestige Paseo de Gracia	opened 2002	Josep Juanpere	16
		Paseo de Gracia, 62	45 rooms including 2 suites	GCA Arquitectos	
		08007 Barcelona	business centre, beauty centre, lounge/bar, restaurant,		
		España	conference facilities		
			located in the centre of Barcelona's arts and financial district		
		www.prestigehotels.com			
Spain	Bilbao	Miró Hotel	opened 2002	Antonio Miró	20
		Alameda Mazarredo, 77	50 rooms including 5 junior suites		
		48009 Bilbao	spa with hammam, jacuzzi and massage		
		España	conference facilities for up to 50 people		
			located between the Guggenheim and the Fine Arts Museum		
		www.hotelmiro.com			

Country / Location		Address	Information	Architecture & Design	Page
France	Paris	Hotel Bel Ami	renovated 2001	Christian Lalande	24
		7-11, rue Saint-Benoît	115 rooms and suites	Nathalie Battesti	
		Saint Germain-des-Prés	meeting place for up to 12 people	Veronique Terreaux	
		75006 Paris	lounge with fireplace, library		
		France	bar, espresso bar		
		www.hotel-bel-ami.com	located at Place Saint-Germain-des-Prés		
France	Paris	Pershing Hall	opened 2001	Andrée Putman	28
		49, rue Pierre Charron	26 rooms and suites		
		75008 Paris	conference facilities for up to 80 people		
		France	restaurant, lounge bar		
			located one step away from the Champs-Elysées		
		www.pershinghall.com	and Av. Montaigne		
France	Paris	Radisson SAS Hotel Champs Elysées	opened 2002	Ecart	32
		78, Avenue Marçeau	46 rooms including 1 suite		
		75008 Paris	restaurant "la place", lounge, wine bar		
		France	located close to the Arc de Triomphe		
		www.radissonsas.com			
Netherlands	Amsterdam	Blakes Hotel	built 1637, renovated 1998	Anouska Hempel	36
		Kreizersgracht 384	26 rooms and 11 suites		
		1016 GB Amsterdam	restaurant, bar		
		Nederlands	conference room for up to 30 people		
			nearby ice skating, sauna, tennis courts		
		www.blakes-amsterdam.com	located 20 min. from Amsterdam Schipol International Airport		
United Kingdom	London	51 Buckingham Gate	built 1901, opened 2002	Dan Nelson	40
		51 Buckingham Gate	82 apartments, including 6 suites	Noel Pierce	
		London SW1E 6AF	restaurants		
		United Kingdom	located in the centre of London, just a 3-minute walk away		
			from Buckingham Palace		
		www.51-buckinghamgate.com			

hotel summary

Country / Location		Address	Information	Architecture & Design	Page
United Kingdom	London	Great Eastern Hotel Liverpool Street London EC2M 7QN United Kingdom www.great-eastern-hotel.co.uk	built 1884, reopened 2000 246 guest rooms and 21 suites conference facilities from 10 to 400 people 4 restaurants, 3 bars fitness centre	Manser Associates CD Partnership Sir Terence Conran James Soane	44
United Kingdom	London	Metropolitan Old Park Lane London W1Y 4LB United Kingdom www.metropolitan.co.uk	opened 1997 155 guest rooms including suites Japanese restaurant Nobu (Michelin starred), Met Bar conference room for up to 50 people walking distance to Picadilly and Knightsbridge	Keith Hobbs Linzi Coppick United Designers	48
United Kingdom	London	No. 5 Maddox No. 5 Maddox Street Mayfair London W1S 2QD United Kingdom www.living-rooms.co.uk	opened 1999 12 suites with private kitchen located in the heart of London, 5 minutes away from Soho and Mayfair	Baker Neville Design	52
United Kingdom	London	Threadneedles Hotel 5 Threadneedles Street London EC2R 8AY United Kingdom www.theetoncollection.com	opened 2002 70 rooms and suites 3 conference and meeting rooms for 8 to 30 people "Bonds" restaurant and bar, salon with "Honey Bar" located close to the Bank of England in the heart of the financial district	GA Design	56
United Kingdom	Manchester	Eleven Didsbury Park Didsbury Village Manchester M2O 5LH United Kingdom www.elevendidsburypark.co.uk	opened 1999 14 guestrooms conference room for up to 14 people Victorian walled garden with hot tub located in fashionable Didsbury	Sally O'Loughlin	60

Country / Location		Address	Information	Architecture & Design	Page
Ireland	Dublin	The Morrison Hotel	opened 1999	John Rocha	64
		Ormond Quay	84 Superior rooms, 6 suites and a penthouse	Hugh Wallace	
		Dublin	2 restaurants, "Halo Bar" and the "Café Bar"		
		Ireland	conferencing for up to 100 people		
			Garden Room, also for private cocktail parties or for meetings		
		www.morrisonhotel.ie	located in the heart of the city, overlooking the River Liffey		
Sweden	Stockholm	Berns Hotel	reopened 1987	Olle Rex	68
		P.O. Box 16340	65 rooms including 4 suites	Terence Conran	
		103 27 Stockholm	10 conference rooms for groups up to 1000 people		
		Sverige	restaurant, lounge bar, cocktail bar, wine bar, nightclub,		
			2 private dining rooms		
		www.berns.se	located close to the Berzelii Park in the heart of Stockholm		
Sweden	Stockholm	Hotel J	opened 2000	Millimeter	72
		Ellensviksvägen 1	45 rooms	R.O.O.M.	
		131 27 Nacka Strand/Stockholm	fitness centre, sauna close by the hotel	Klas Litzén	
		Sverige	located 10-15 minutes from Stockholm by car or boat	Nirén	
		www.hotelj.com			
Germany	Hamburg	Gastwerk Hotel	opened 2000	Klaus Peter Lange	76
		Beim Alten Gaswerk 3 / Daimlerstr.	135 rooms including 10 suites	Regine Schwethelm	
		22761 Hamburg	conference and meeting centre with 5 conference rooms	Sybille von Heyden	
		Deutschland	Italian restaurant "Da Caio"		
			winter garden, sauna, relaxation zone		
		www.gastwerk-hotel.de	located 10-15 minutes from city centre and harbour		
Germany	Hamburg	SIDE Hotel	opened 2001	Florian Störmer	80
		Drehbahn 49	156 rooms, 12 junior suites and 10 suites	Alsop Störmer	
		20354 Hamburg	6 conference rooms including executive lounge on 8th floor	Matteo Thun	
		Deutschland	"Fusion" restaurant and bar	Robert Wilson	
			spa with pool, sauna, fitness centre, body treatments		
		www.seaside-hotels.de	located near the Alster river and the opera house		

hotel summary

Country / Location		Address	Information	Architecture & Design	Page
Germany	Berlin	Dorint Am Gendarmenmarkt	opened 1999	Harald Klein	86
		Charlottenstr. 50-52	92 rooms including 21 suites	Bert Haller	
		10117 Berlin	restaurant, bar, rooftop terrace	K/H Büro für Design und Innenarchitektur	
		Deutschland	sauna, steam bath, wellness area with terrace, fitness centre		
			6 conference rooms for up to 120 people		
		www.dorint.de/berlin-gendarmenmarkt/	right around government district and most important sights		
Germany	Berlin	Ku'damm101	opened 2003	Eyl, Weitz, Würmle & Partner	90
		Kurfürstendamm 101	171 rooms	Kadel-Quick-Scheib	
		10711 Berlin	5 conference rooms for up to 120 people	Kessler + Kessler	
		Deutschland	3 conference suites for up to 12 people	Lemongras Design Studio, Gruppe-RE	
			breakfast restaurant, lounge bar, catering service	Vogt + Weizenegger	
		www.kudamm101.com	located at the Kurfüstendamm in Berlin's shopping district	Lützow 7	
Germany	Cologne	Hopper St. Antonius	opened 1999	Rolf Kursawe	94
		Dagobertstr. 32	54 guest rooms (small, medium, large und x-large)		
		50668 Köln	Spitz restaurant		
		Deutschland	2 conference rooms for up to 20 people		
			located in the city centre		
		www.hopper.de			
Germany	Munich	Cortiina	opened 2001	Albert Weinzierl	98
		Ledererstr. 8	33 rooms		
		80331 München	located in the historical city centre, just a few minutes away		
		Deutschland	from opera, theatres and the Hofbräuhaus		
		www.cortiina.com			
Czech Republic	Prague	Hotel Josef	opened 2002	Eva Jiricna	102
		Rybna 20	110 rooms		
		110 00 Prag 1	breakfast restaurant, bar		
		Česká Republika	3 conference rooms up to 90 people		
			located in the centre of Prague, a 5-minute walk away from		
		www.hoteljosef.com	the historical city centre		

Country / Location		Address	Information	Architecture & Design	Page
Austria	Vienna	Das Triest	opened 1995	Peter Lorenz	106
		Wiedner Hauptstr. 12	59 guest rooms, 13 suites	CD Partnership	
		1040 Wien	2 conference rooms up to 120 people	Sir Terence Conran	
		Österreich	70 seat restaurant, The Silver Bar	James Soane	
			fitness centre with sauna and solarium		
		www.dastriest.at	located in the city, 10 minutes walk to St. Stephans Cathedral		
Austria	Graz	Augarten Hotel	opened 2000	Günther Domenig	110
		Schöngaugasse 53	36 rooms,20 apartments		
		8010 Graz	3 conference rooms		
		Österreich	restaurant, 24-hour bar		
			indoor pool and sun terrace, sauna, solarium, fitness room		
		www.augartenhotel.at	view across Graz from the roof-top terrace		
Switzerland	Zurich	Greulich	opened 2003	Romero & Schaefle	114
		Herman-Greulich-Str. 56	10 rooms, 8 junior suites	Jean Pfaff	
		8004 Zürich	restaurant, bar, cigar lounge	Günther Vogt	
		Schweiz	conference facilities for up to 30 people		
			located 2 km from the city centre		
		www.greulich.ch			
Switzerland	Zürich	Widder Hotel	opened 1995	Tilla Theus	118
		Rennweg 7	42 guest rooms, 7 suites		
		8001 Zürich	4 restaurants, "Widder Bar"		
		Schweiz	7 meeting rooms from 8 to 200 people		
			located in the city centre		
		www.designhotels.com			
Switzerland	Lucerne	The Hotel	opened 2000	Jean Nouvel	122
		Sempacherstr. 14	25 rooms including 10 Garden & Park Deluxe suites,		
		6002 Luzern	10 Deluxe studios and 5 Corner Junior studios		
		Schweiz	hip bar "The Lounge", stylish restaurant "Bam Bou"		
			located in the heart of Lucerne		
		www.the-hotel.ch			

hotel summary

Country / Location		Address	Information	Architecture & Design	Page
Italy	Bolzano	Hotel Greif Waltherplatz 39100 Bolzano Italia www.greif.it	opened 2000 33 rooms, each furnished by its own artist at the nearby Parkhotel Laurin under same operation: park and pool, garden restaurant, Laurin Bar with piano music, meeting and banquet facilities for up to 180 people located in the historical city centre of Bolzano	Boris Podrecca	126
Italy	Milan	The Gray Via San Raffaele, 6 20121 Milano Italia www.sinahotels.com	opened 2003 21 rooms and suites located between the dome and La Scala, opposite to the recently renovated Galleria Vittorio Emanuelle	Guido Ciompi	130
Italy	Cremona	Delle Arti Design Hotel Via Bonomelli, 8 26100 Cremona Italia www.dellearti.com	opened 2002 33 rooms including 2 suites and 1 apartment meeting and conferencing facilities for up to 28 people located in the historical city centre	Michele Bonan	134
Italy	Florence	Hotel Continentale Vicolo dell'Oro 6r 50123 Firenze Italia www.lungarnohotels.com	opened 2003 43 rooms including 1 penthouse suite bar, roof-top sun deck, fitness centre located at Ponte Vecchio view from the rooms on the river Arno	Michele Bonan	138
Italy	Florence	Gallery Hotel Art Vicolo dell'Oro 5 50123 Firenze Italia www.lungarnohotels.com	opened 1999 60 guest rooms, 2 duplex suites, 2 penthouse suites, 1 junior suite Fusion Bar Shozan Gallery with terrace library, nearby fitness centre located a few steps from the Ponte Vecchio	Michele Bonan	142

Country / Location		Address	Information	Architecture & Design	Page
Italy	Venice	Ca' Pisani	opened 2000	Roberto Luigi Canovaro	146
		Dorsoduro 979/a	30 rooms and suites	Pierluigi Pescolderung	
		Rio Tera' Antonio Foscarini	cheese and wine bar "La Rivista" with terrace		
		30123 Venezia	art gallery		
		Italia	located in the Accademia district, just a few minutes from		
		www.capisanihotel.it	the Canal Grande		
Italy	Rome	Hotel Art	opened 2003	Raniero Botti	150
		Via Margutta 56	49 rooms including 2 suites	Gianfranco Mangiarotti	
		00187 Roma	lounge, bar, breakfast room		
		Italia	fitness centre with sauna and hammam		
			located in the city at the Piazza Spagna, 10 minutes from		
		www.slh.com/hotelart	Piazza del Popolo and Fontana di Trevi		
Turkey	Istanbul	Bentley Hotel	opened 2003	Piero Lissoni	154
		Halaskargazi Cad. No. 75, Harbiye	40 rooms and suites	Nicoletta Canesi	
		80220 Istanbul	lobby bar, mezzanine restaurant, private dining areas		
		Türkiye	conference room for up to 14 people		
			located in the city centre, 5 minutes from the shopping area		
		www.bentley-hotel.com	view from Bosporus to the Golden Horn		

architects & designers

photo credits

Other photography by

Roland Bauer (51 Buckingham Gate, The Gray, Greulich,
Metropolitan, Pershing Hall, Radisson SAS, Threadneedles Hotel),
Martin N. Kunz (Hotel Art, Hotel Claris, The Gray, Prestige)

Verana, Puerto Vallarta, Mexico · photography by Heinz Legler

wellness
for the eyes

Wellness is a keyword for our times. But only
seldom are wellness programmes presented in
conjunction with an esthetic environment. These
books present a collection of some of the most
fascinating properties in Asia/Pacific, the Americas
and Europe, that combine outstanding wellness
facilities with the finest in architecture and design.
Whether in harmony with the environment, or in
deliberate contrast to the landscape, these hotels
and resorts offer the best of a new global breed.

best designed wellness hotels
India · South East Asia · Australia · Pacific

ISBN: 3-929638-91-6
168 pages, hardcover
published: May 2002

best designed wellness hotels
Northern & Southern America · Caribbean

ISBN: 3-929638-87-8
168 pages, hardcover
published: November 2002

best designed wellness hotels
West- und Mitteleuropa · Alpen · Mittelmeer

ISBN: 3-929638-85-1
168 pages, hardcover
published: May 2003

**available at selected book stores
or at www.avedition.com**

avedition **lebensart**

imprint

Bibliographic information published by Die Deutsche Bibliothek Die Deutsche Bibliothek lists this publication in the Deutsche Nationalbibliografie; detailed bibliographic data are available in the Internet at http://dnb.ddb.de

ISBN 3-89986-001-2

Printed in Germany

Publisher I Martin Nicholas Kunz
Translations I Andrea Adelung, Vineeta Manglani
Editing I Sally Hayden, Scott Michael Crouch
Texts (page) I Frank Bantle (52,134), Ursula Dietmair (154), Sibylle Eck (64), Claudia El Ahwani (110, 122, 126), Benjamin A. Finn (28, 40, 68,98, 142), Inna Hartwich (S. 16, 20), Bärbel Holzberg (24, 26, 32, 36, 150), Ina Sinterhauf (60, 72, 94, 146), Heinfried Tacke (56, 102, 114).
All other texts by Martin N. Kunz
Research I Patricia Massó, Ulrike Paul
Art Direction I Dorothee Hübner, Patricia Müller
Printing I Leibfarth & Schwarz GmbH & Co KG, Dettingen/Erms

Special Thanks to: Eva Bardel, Augarten Hotel, Graz I Elke Balkhausen, Hopper St. Antonius I Jan E. Brucker, Widder Hotel, Zurich I Thomas B. Brunner, Greulich, Zurich I Glenn Caroll, Metropolitan, London I Victoria Woelpl, Cortiina, Munich I Emmanuelle Coutat, Hotel Bel Ami, Paris I Silvio Lacchini, Delle Arti Design Hotel, Cremona I Murat Ercan, Bentley Hotel, Istanbul I Sabina Galdiolo, Sina Hotels I Vanessa Giovannelli, Lungarno Hotels I Jens Gmiat, Ku'damm101, Berlin I Doris Gotter, Hotel Greif, Bozen I Anne-Claire Goutal, GLA International I Fernando Gruenberg Stern, SAS Radisson Champs Elysées I Anouska Hempel, Blakes, Amsterdam I Maria Hessedahl, Hotel J, Stockholm I Kai Hollmann, Gastwerk Hotel, Hamburg I Bärbel Holzberg, Munich I Mikael Landström, Portixol, Mallorca I Urs Langenegger, The Hotel, Lucerne I Antonio Miró, Miró Hotel, Bilbao I Giuliano Nardiotii, The Gray, Milan I Kevin Nicholas, The Eton Group, London I Joachim Olausson, Berns Hotel, Stockholm I Eamon O'Loughlin, Eleven Didsbury Park, Manchester I Victor Philipps, No. 5 Maddox, London I Ana Pons, Hotel Claris, Barcelona I Tini Gräfin Rothkirch, Dorint Am Gendarmenmarkt, Berlin I Natalia Ruiz, Prestige Paseo de Gracia, Barcelona I Maria Samoy, Livingrooms, London I Paula Scallon, The Morrison Hotel, Dublin I Marianna und Gianni Serandrei, Ca' Pisani, Venice I Manfred Stalmajer, Das Triest, Vienna I Ronald Starke, SIDE Hotel, Hamburg I Tilla Theus, Zurich I Manfred Tobolka, Hotel Josef, Prague I Beverly Visco, Pershing Hall, Paris I Simon Willis, Great Eastern Hotel, London

Martin Nicholas Kunz

Born 1957 in Hollywood. Martin is responsible for communications and publishing at lebensart global networks AG. Martin worked as an editor for several German and other international magazines such as "design report" and was Managing Director of New Media for the German publisher DVA, a company known for its architecture, design and craft books, magazines and web sites. He is author and co-author of several design, craft and construction books, and since 2001, author and publisher of the avedition lebensart book series "best designed..."; seven books of the world's most beautiful hotels.

avedition GmbH
Königsallee 57 I 71638 Ludwigsburg I Germany
p +49-7141-1477391 I f +49-7141-1477399
http://www.avedition.de I info@avedition.de